Russian Revolution

The Russian Revolution From Beginning To End

(The History Of The Russian Empire's Collapse And The Establishment Of The Soviet Union)

Rudy Rickman

Published By **Jackson Denver**

Rudy Rickman

All Rights Reserved

Russian Revolution: The Russian Revolution From Beginning To End (The History Of The Russian Empire's Collapse And The Establishment Of The Soviet Union)

ISBN 978-1-77485-634-5

No part of this guidebook shall be reproduced in any form without permission in writing from the publisher except in the case of brief quotations embodied in critical articles or reviews.

Legal & Disclaimer

The information contained in this ebook is not designed to replace or take the place of any form of medicine or professional medical advice. The information in this ebook has been provided for educational & entertainment purposes only.

The information contained in this book has been compiled from sources deemed reliable, and it is accurate to the best of the Author's knowledge; however, the Author cannot guarantee its accuracy and validity and cannot be held liable for any errors or omissions. Changes are periodically made to this book. You must consult your doctor or get professional medical advice before using any of the suggested remedies, techniques, or information in this book.

Upon using the information contained in this book, you agree to hold harmless the Author from and against any damages, costs, and expenses, including any legal fees potentially resulting from the application of any of the information provided by this guide. This disclaimer applies to any damages or injury caused by the use and application, whether directly or indirectly, of any advice or information presented, whether for breach of contract, tort, negligence, personal injury, criminal intent, or under any other cause of action.

You agree to accept all risks of using the information presented inside this book. You need to consult a professional medical practitioner in order to ensure you are both able and healthy enough to participate in this program.

Table Of Contents

Introduction 1

Chapter 1: Timeline Of Events 6

Chapter 2: Background Of The Russian Revolution 14

Chapter 3: The Revolution Begins...27

Chapter 4: The Return Of Lenin 39

Chapter 5: The October Revolution 50

Chapter 6: Early History (800-1200). 55

Chapter 7: Tsardom In Russia (1500-1500). 71

Chapter 8: Imperial Russia, 1800 - 1900 86

Chapter 9: The Russian Revolution (And The Creation Of The Soviet Union)...98

Chapter 10: World War Ii..............118

Chapter 11: Cold War 135

Chapter 12: Russia Today's Breakup Of The Union 145

Introduction

When walking the streets of Saint Petersburg, it is easy to think about its turbulent past. You can't help thinking about the past. There are reminders at every corner, every structure and every landmark. Saint Petersburg was once Petrograd. However, the name was changed in World War I to make it more German. Then it became Leningrad at the death Vladimir Lenin. And then it was returned to Saint Petersburg when the Soviet Union collapsed in 1991. The Hermitage Museum is home to the powerful remains of the Tsars. Russia is no longer an empire. After revolutionaries overthrew Romanov monarchy for over three hundred years, Yekaterinburg saw the brutal execution of the last members o the imperial ruler class.

The Russian revolution not only ended a bloodthirsty dictatorship, but also gave rise to the Soviet Union. It was a period of massive uprisings that included high-profile assassinations. Lenin was born in Russia during the Russian Revolution. Stalin also emerged from this revolution. There are many places where you can see Lenin's statues, whether you travel across Russia or

Europe. Lenin is credited as the hero for the creation the powerful Soviet Union. His preserved body is on display at Moscow's Red Square, where it can be viewed in the Lenin Mausoleum. This impressive and important necropolis is open to public viewing for five days each week.

Lenin may be the hero behind the major moves that saw Lenin's fall, but he is not the only one. Some believe that the courage of the Bolsheviks' soldiers and common workers helped lead to Vladimir Ilyich Ulyanov's victory and the rise of Vladimir Ilyich Ulyanov. Lenin's co-conspirators supervised the birth of one among the most powerful civil countries. They were led by Karl Marx's ideology and rode on the tide of discontent and activism of millions of people who had endured decades of oppression.

A Russian Revolution was centered around a royal household that was quickly becoming the target of severe criticism for its blunders, and other failures throughout the years. The situation did not improve with the onset of World War I and Russia's extensive defeats by the Germans. Thousands upon countless of ordinary people and revolutionaries died either fighting against the monarchy or protesting it. This was a time in which ordinary citizens could have small arms and create improvised explosions. In fact, several assassinations or attempted assassinations targeting the royals and other prominent members were made with improvised explosions. Tsar Alexander was attacked in one the most violent and graphic assassinations that took place during the first stages of the Russian Revolution. Aleksandr Ulyanov "Sasha", Lenin's older brother, was later executed after attempting to assassinate Alexander II. He is also remembered for his early Marxist-inspired ideologies which fuelled the anti-imperial activism. His execution inspired the man who is now known to have founded the Soviet Union, to take the revolutionary path even though he was at risk of experiencing the same fate.

The Russian Empire lost a number of wars under the leadership of the tsars starting in the 1800s. They went into war with Japan in Crimea. They lost. After that, they entered World War I. Nicholas II became the military strategist. His performance was poor. These terrible wars were what the Bolsheviks worried about, among other issues. These and other bad choices, including

Rasputin's participation with Tsarina, left the tsars vulnerable to revolution.

The Bolsheviks victory brought the empire down and eventually led directly to its destruction. The Soviet Union was the place where Communism was established. Its influence spread throughout the globe. The Russian Revolution's importance went far beyond its humble goals, such as protecting workers' rights, to total radicalism that resulted in a civil battle that killed more than 15,000 Russians. It was perhaps the most brutal and unromantic revolutions recorded in the history Europe. Although so much was happening between 1905 and 1920, one cannot help but to recall the horrific killing by firing squad in Yekaterinburg which claimed the lives of the whole royal family. Lenin ordered the bloody executions.

Joseph Vissarionovich Stalin. Have you ever heard of them? I'm sure you have. He led the Soviet Union during the two decades following the death of Lenin. Stalin was introduced at the height of the revolution to Lenin and quickly became one of his closest confidants within the Kremlin. He was a key figure that worked in the shadows when Lenin & the Bolsheviks retook power from a provisional government. His reign would end in disappointment for many and become a dictatorship of brutal totalitarianism and repression that led to unimaginable horrors such ethnic cleansing.

Here is the story of Russia's Revolution as seen from 21st Century perspective. Contrary the past's narratives, statements and beliefs, the Russian Revolution didn't happen in a single year. Nor was it about Lenin, the Bolsheviks, as some have claimed. The history of this revolution is tied to previous tsars (from Alexander II to his successor and finally Nicholas II and the disastrous Tsarina) and the events of September 1905, which was swiftly defeated by the empire. Some may argue that Lenin and his accomplices took advantage a situation that was already developing. Lenin, his group and the Kerensky government were able to seize power from them. They had already gotten rid the monarchy. We'll examine the stories before, during and afterwards the Russian uprising.

Chapter 1: Timeline of Events

The January Strikes (industrial actions)

A general strike is called for by more than 100,000 workers to commemorate the 1905 Bloody Sunday massacre.

February--Start for the Revolution

The advisory and legislative assembly (Duma), launches an adamant attack on the Imperial government for not addressing the serious food shortage. Most workers, including rail and postal workers, are still striking.

February 19--Foodration by the Tsarist State

In an effort to make an already desperate situation even worse, government introduces food restriction in order to prevent extreme food shortages. This leads to widespread discontent among the population as people rush in panic to buy as much food before the rationing starts.

February 23 - Mass Action in Support of International Women's Day

International Women's Day marks the culmination of the largest public demonstrations against Nicholas's regime. Many protestors, mostly women and large groups take over Petrograd and other major cities. Other anti-government protesters, as well as socialists, join the demonstrations. There are many fatal clashes with authorities.

Violent Protests & Police Brutality

Petrograd and other cities continue to witness public demonstrations, with the number of protestors increasing each day. As the number of protesters increases, there are more clashes with authorities. The culmination is an order to shoot at Nicholas II. In broad daylight many protestors are killed and shot by police.

Nicholas II, who is agitated, orders to disintegrate the Duma. This order is ignored and some soldiers rebel against their commanders in disobedience of the tsar's shoot-to–kill order. This is when the rebellious garrisons of the murderous Tsarist government began to revolt. In the later stages of the revolution, the crucial role played by armed soldiers will play a major part. These events are the catalyst for the Petrograd Soviet's formation.

The Plotting Begins

The Duma meets the Petrograd Soviet for a series to discuss strategies to overthrow his government. Nicholas's attempt is to travel to Petrograd when he encounters delays at the railway station. These delays are either caused by striking railway workers, or by orders of the Petrograd Soviet. To take over the failing tsarist state, a provisional government was established.

The Tsar's Assassination

Tsar Nicholas abdicates after facing widespread opposition and increasing support from anti-tsarist voices. Grand Duke Michael accepts the throne but refuses to take it unless it is mandated by his assembly brother. The provisional government that was newly formed takes control of the country, ending 300 years worth of Romanov rule in Russia Empire.

Recognition of Provisional Governance by Foreign Powers

After the creation of the provisional administration, foreign leaders, such as British and French leaders acknowledged it to be the official government of Russia. This marks a turning point in Russia's history, with the dissolution of the tsarist government.

Provisional Government Reforms

As expected, the provisional governments introduces radical reforms that are meant to lower the burden on the masses. New laws cover assembly elections as well civil liberties and freedoms and the pardoning or release of political prisoners.

Nicholas II Detention and His Family

After the removal of the royals from office, the provisional administration placed them under house arrest. They will be subject to trial and possibly execution. Although the new civil government of revolutionaries has taken control of the state, it is still unclear what the state's problems are. There are still protests and civil warfare.

The Death Penalty Has been Abolished

The provisional governments are implementing reforms which include the elimination of the death penalty. To eliminate dissidents or activists, the tsarists have used the death sentence for decades. This move is meant both to make the provisional government more popular and to provide self-preservation for some radicals in the government who overthrew his regime.

Lenin returns

After being tortured and beaten by the Okhrana for over 16 year, Lenin found himself in exile. He is determined to come back to Russia to carry on his revolutionary efforts. With the help of Germans, they take a treacherous train ride back to Russia. He arrives at the train station and makes an emotional speech. This speech will later become the foundation of the revolutionary ideologies known as the April Movement (April Theses). He is about the takeover of the Bolshevik movements that will eventually overthrow Kerensky's provisional regime.

The July Days Mass Demonstrations

With Lenin's return, the Bolsheviks have more support from the people and soldiers disgruntled at the economic situation and Russia's involvement with World War I. Mass protests are organized against the provisional regime, prompting Pavel Nikolayevich Milyukov's resignation and Aleksandr Kerensky's takeover.

Kerensky takes a sharp attack on Lenin. He accuses him in a series of offences against the provisional regime. He is also charged with being an agent of Germans, who protected his exile. Lenin is forced by this to flee Finland to avoid persecution from the Kerensky government. Bolsheviks as well as soldiers rebelling against the provisional government are quickly stopped and sent to prison.

The Failed Austro-Hungarian Offensive

Aleksandr Kerensky orders against Austro Hungarian force an offensive that leads to defeat and thousands Russian casualties. Bolsheviks, who oppose the war, become more determined as they demand a peaceful resolution to Russia's disastrous involvement in WWI.

The Reintroduction of the Penalty for Death

Kerensky faces increasing pressure from top army officers and others in the provisional administration to reinstate the death penalty, due to the growing number of military deserters. Kerensky will have no choice but to comply with the order on July 12th.

Significant Changing of the Guard at the Military

Lavr Georgiyevich Kornilov becomes a radical figure and takes the Russian military's control from Aleksei Brusilov. He marches his soldiers to Petrograd to retake power from the "Socialists" in what will later be known as The Kornilov Affair. Although it was meant to support the Kerensky government, it is misinterpreted by many as a coup that backfires. Kornilov is detained by the same government that he was trying raise and sent into prison. A few months later Kornilov is freed by the same government and sent to prison. He then enlists in the White Army.

The Strike of the Railway Employees

Kerensky-led government comes under increasing pressure. As thousands of railway workers abandon their positions, the transport system in Russia is paralysed. (The railway system and the postal service were vital institutions in Russia early in the 20th century. Some Bolsheviks imprisoned during Lenin's rebellion against the provisional state were freed by strikes.

The October Revolution

Lenin, however, is still hiding. He works in the background alongside the Bolsheviks. Bolsheviks hold the majority of assembly members and are able to seize power from Kerenskys. Leon Trotsky a Marxist is appointed chairman. The Bolsheviks then make moves to take power and launch attacks upon key members in the provisional government. Most of them are detained and sent to jail. Kerensky however manages escape to Pskov, and later to Paris.

Lenin's Rise

Lenin, now in control of the government, forms the Soviet government, eliminates all remnants to the tsarist systems, supervises the reform process and holds elections. Vladimir Ilyich Ulyanov aka Lenin is a Soviet Russian ruler who reigns for nearly a decade. In 1924, he succumbs a blood vessel condition that causes him to go into a coma. The dictator-in chief, Stalin.

Chapter 2: Background of the Russian Revolution

The Russian Revolution in 1917 began as a 1905 revolution. This revolution was easily neutralized with the help of the tsar. Revolutions such as those in the Russian Revolution and even the Cuban Revolution did not originate from anywhere. Most of the revolutions in the world share one thing, namely, famine. Russian Revolution was the result years of bad decisions of a repressive, authoritarian monarchy which had put the common people at the edge.

Russia was not developed in the early 20th-century. Most Russians were either poor peasants in a declining economy and under bad land law, or civil servants in dire conditions within various government institutions. But the tsars, and other key government figures, had everything they could need in their lives. They lived in grand palaces and traveled abroad for their own pleasure.

A growing number educated ideologists, like Lenin were also trying to get rid of the tsarists. The revolutionaries from tsarist Russia looked nothing like the ones in other European countries. They were ready and willing to take the war to royalty via repeated assassination attempts, fatal clashes on the streets, and other means. Bombs were used with mixed success to assassinate unpopular rulers.

Alexander II was a reformist tsar and succumbed to the radical revolutionaries, known as the People's Will or Narodnaya Volya. Alexander II of Russia was well-known for his radical reforms in the areas of the judiciary, corporal punishment and keeping the nobility in line. He was a favorite tsar. His leadership of Russia and Poland lasted more than two decades. The tsar responsible for selling Alaska to America in 1867 may be well-known to Americans.

The reign of Tsar Alexander II Russia was at a time when discontent was high and there was a strong activist movement to eliminate the tsarist systems. The revolver was popularized by radicals in Russia at that time. It is a small lethal weapon capable of firing several bullets and can be used to kill. Radical revolutionaries, at the time terrorists and enemies against the empire, also had their own explosives manufacturing business.

Three assassinations attempted on Tsar Alexander II II Russia to his core were successful.

Alexander Soloviev was a student who attempted to assassinate Alexander. This happened in April 1879. Soloviev only managed five shots from his revolver to the tsar and his guards at a St Petersburg square. The gunman was not able to kill the tsar. Alexander Soloviev died later. He did not associate himself and his actions with radical "People's Will."

In December 2002, Tsar Alexander II II was subject to another assassination attempt. The radical "People's Will," revolutionaries in Ukraine had planned on blowing up the train carrying the tsar. They were not precise enough and managed to destroy a freight truck.

The third and greatest assassination attempt was in February 2001. This attack shook the entire establishment and shocked the tsar. The People's Will, determined that they would execute their self declared death sentence upon the tsar executed a much larger dynamite load below a Winter Palace restaurant where Tsar Alexander II was due to have dinner with his family as well as other dignitaries. He was not present in the dining hall at the time of the explosion due to delays. Many guards and other victims were also killed in the blast. This attempted attack on his life completely shaken the tsar and he took an extended hiatus from attending important public events.

While a cat is believed to have nine lives (but Tsar Alexander II, Russia's ruler, only had four. However, the People's Will had not finished their assassination efforts. In March 1881 (1881), they succeeded.

It was in the early morning of February 13, 1881. The Russian Tsar Alexander II was accompanied by heavy security, riding in a bulletproof carriage donated by Napoleon III. He was on his route to the routine military call he loved at Michael Manege. This time, the People's Will revolutionaries devised a redundancy scheme to ensure the death of the tsar.

As they were approaching the Pevcheskybridge, along the narrow Catherine Canal a member from the People's Will called Nikolai Rysakov began to throw an explosive device. It completely immobilized Alexander II of Russia's bulletproof carriage. This was just another failed attempt at assassination. Both you and I know it wasn't. However, this is not what Alexander II of Russia thought at time. Nikolai Rysakov having been neutralized and Nikolai Rysakov safely out of his carriage, the Tsar went on to inspect the scene, despite being urged not to by the police.

Little did they know, there were still two People's Will bombers in the crowd next to the canal. IgnacyHryniewiecki created the second explosion that killed tsar and was believed to be history's first suicide bomber. This second explosion destroyed the body of the tsar, completely immobilizing it. It is believed that the tsar saw his body cut in half. His lower legs were completely blown off, exploding and exposing his intestines. It's a miracle that he was able, despite thinking it was a minor incident, to call the police chief who was there to assist him. Sergey Petrovich Botkin arrived at his Winter Palace office to examine him and he later succumbed.

The majority of People's Will's members were later imprisoned or executed, but their actions as well as ideologies shaped the foundation for the later revolutionaries. Most historians ignore 19th-century Russia's events under Tsar Alexander 2 and dismiss People's Will as a radical group. However, those who were later released carried on the movement which later became a fully fledged revolution. His father was brutally assassinated, and the next tsar would go on to be a brutal dictator. Aleksandr III Aleksandrovich would be his name. Alexander III of Russia is his common title.

Russia under Alexander III & How Nicholas II Came Into Being

It is important to mention Alexander III of Russia's reign as well as how his relationship to Nicholas II may have contributed to 1917's abolitionists of the Romanov throne. Although his father was a reformist who supervised many changes that were intended to make life easier and to improve the lives of his subjects, Alexander II was forced through his predecessor's assassination into a new, unpopular way to lead.

The new Tsar decided to crack down on radical groups, which were seen as enemies to the monarchy. Alexander III was a massive man with strong physical features. He was also a forceful character and always got his way. He reversed many of the father's reforms. He also restored the rule of the ruling classes' autocracy. Alexander III also elevated the land captains, ensuring he regained control in the nobility. He made it mandatory that Russian was taught in all schools.

Alexander III was also known as a good manager of the Russian economic system. He was a strong advocate of the industrialization in Russia and made major improvements to the railway system. He was responsible for rapid modernizations of important infrastructure in Russia, though it was done through autocratic means. Alexander III's rule denied the working class, nobility, or peasants any outlet for their opinions. His style of leadership and personal character reflected the belief of the tsars, that they were bound by a God given obligation to control the country without civil rights or democracy. He was a good ruler, but he was also repressive.

Tsar Alexander III also goes by the name of the Peacemaker because he never went into war with other countries during his reign. By signing treaties and settlements, and employing diplomacy as appropriate, he was capable of avoiding potential conflicts against Great Britain and Germany. Potential aggressors who feared defeat from France's combined military might and the Russian Empire would be deterred by his agreement with France.

Aleksandr Ulyanov Lenin's elder son, Aleksandr Ulyanov joined forces with some of the People's Will terrorists to plan another assassination. However, their plot was foiled by the secret cops who discovered it before they could carry out the execution.

Aleksandr Ulyanov had a reputation for being a diligent fellow. He studied Marxist ideologies extensively and used them to develop the faction's ideas. He believed that the state should have a middle class as its foundation and was against autocratic government. Aleksandr Ulyanov with five others were sentenced to death for plotting the assassination. Lenin learned of the fate and determination of his brother, and decided to take a personal vendetta at the tsarists.

If we look at Nicholas II's family life, we can see why he failed as a leader. Alexander III was not fondly acquainted with Nicholas Tsarevich Nicholas II (Nicholas II), while he was still a child. Because of his intimidating figure and repressiveness, the young lad became less interested and more detached in the day to-day running the state under his father. His father had died at the age of 26 and he left him behind.

Nicholas II, like Louis XVI (France) in the 18th Century, was completely inept at fulfilling his duties. He instead relied solely on his "Godgiven" mandate, much to both his own safety and the ruin of the monarchy. Tsar Alexander IV died in 1894 at age 49 due to sudden kidney failure. This may have been caused perhaps by an earlier incident he had with family members.

Nicholas II, the Fall of the Monarchy

After his coronation May 26, 1896, Nicholas II, Tsar Nicholas II started his reign on a very bad note. The tradition of a public banquet was established by every new tsar. This is where the royals would give out gifts to commoners. This ceremony took part on May 30, 1896. It ended in a tragedy that left over 1,000 people dead.

There had been a large gathering in the field, waiting for coronation festivities. The rumors of a shortage of gifts were false and there was some misinformation about which gift packs they would receive. This created anxiety among the crowd of over half a thousand. It was clear that there was no way for the tsar to feed all these people.

Police were called to handle the panicked crowd. Over a 1000 people were killed or seriously injured. Nicholas II wasn't aware of the situation. He went on with his speech-making and the banquet as usual when he arrived. It wasn't until much later that he was informed. These and other blunders caused a severe damage to the monarchy's reputation, which in turn fueled the revolution. To mark the sad event, today's elegant Orthodox church can be found in the middle Khodynka.

The Unpopular Tsarina

Tsar Nicholas 2 was not only hated by his repressive policies. His foreign spouse, who seemed to be managing the state's affairs from the background, was equally dislikable. Many revolutionaries considered her a negative figure because she was originally from Germany, a country at odds with Russia. Alexandra Feodorovna also was hated for her connection with Grigori Rusputin, a mystic-healer who she had invited into their home to cure their son of hemophilia.

Rumours have it that Grigori Raputin was involved with the tsarina. His involvement is believed to have had an influence on the decisions of Nicholas 2 in the background. Many historians have identified his presence as the reason the monarchy fell. Rasputin survived several stabbing attempts and was later murdered by a group composed of nobles. His body was shot up and thrown in the Malaya Nevka River. The monarchy fell a few short weeks later.

Alexandra Feodorovna was an alien and struggled to connect with Russians. It was a disgrace that she didn't come from an Orthodox family, spoke no Russian fluently, and could not produce a healthy heir to the tsar. Her first four daughters were all girls. Her fifth child, hemophilia, was an incurable and terrible condition. That is why Grigori Rassiin was necessary.

Bloody Sunday

Bloody Sunday was a significant event that occurred in the heat after the failed 1905 uprisings. The reputation of Tsar Nicholas II, one of the most prominent 1905 uprisings leaders, plummeted to the lowest possible levels. Tsar Nicholas 2 stupidly ordered the slaughter of thousands upon thousands of protesters lining up to his St. Petersburg palace, to present a petition. This was one moment in monarchy's lowest hour and probably one of key triggers of mass actions for the months and subsequent years.

On Bloody Sunday more than 200 unarmed protestors were gunned down by the Imperial Guard. An additional 300 were left with serious injuries. More than 6,000 were taken into police custody and sentenced to jail. The tsar may not have managed to end the 1905 revolution but he only fueled the fire that was already setting the stage for the destruction of the monarchy. Nicholas the bloody was soon the nickname of most anti-imperialists.

"I will never consent to a representative type of government because that would be detrimental to the people God entrusted to me Tsar Nicholas 2, 1904

Those were his words when he was confronted by repeated calls for reforms to the form of governance. The Duma was actually created by the Tsar during the initial stages of the 1905 Revolution, but its powers are very limited. It wasn't what people wanted but the newly established state Duma, which was a product of the 1905 Revolution, would play an important role in the penultimate revolutionary of 1917.

Bloody Sunday sparked distrust in the middle classes and peasants that had for decades trusted the monarchy. In the aftermath of the Bloody Sunday events, there were large demonstrations in the major cities. Workers from the middle class went on strike. Nicholas II took forceful action and had thousands imprisoned and executed striking workers. The tsar did eventually defeat the revolutionaries but lost all credibility among the common folks. It was only a matter of time until he was forced to abdicate because of larger uprisings.

Chapter 3: The Revolution Begins

Russia would experience a true revolution ten-years after the failed 1905 revolts. It would mark the end of a 300 years-old dynasty as well as the establishment of the Soviet Union. Different ideologies would be fighting for control in a state that was in despair and war. Russia's disastrous World War I commitments to allies would lead to thousands of soldiers leaving their posts and creating an anti-monarchy political group called the Petrograd Stalin.

On the other hand of the divide, the Mensheviks or Bolsheviks existed. The constituting of the representative assemblies would play an important role in the creation a civil state after the abolition the monarchy.

Russia was a long way behind Europe's major economies when it began the 20th century. The vast majority of Russians worked in fast-growing cities or as peasants on the land. They had the challenge of navigating unfair land ownership laws. Only a small fraction of fertile lands was owned and controlled by poor peasants. All the rest was owned either by the monarchy or the aristocracy. Due to rapid industrialization as well as overpopulation, urban infrastructure was in terrible shape. In the big cities and in industrial towns, there were many unattended sewer pipes, dirty streets, and poorly built homes.

Then, there were the wars of Europe which devasted Russia's economic and created severe food and other hardships in the countryside and in the cities. Thousands of soldiers, men and women were forced to join the army and suffered terrible injuries fighting against a German military that was far more advanced. Most of those who survived developed deep resentment for the monarchy and many would vote against it in the following months and even days.

Tsar Nicholas I, who adhered to the conservative idea of leading from front, declared himself a military strategist as well as commander in Chief in World War I. His mistake would soon come back to haunt him. Following the orders of his tsar thousands of Russian soldiers marched into battle in World War I. Germany won most of the encounters. Many Russians, including soldiers who were affected, held the tsar personally liable for the war's failures.

Russia's failing transportation system was partly responsible for a devastating famine. Due to severe disruptions in rail networks and autarkical tendencies by rural peasants in 1916, little food was able to reach urban areas in sufficient quantities and at the right moment. The majority of the land in the area was owned by the wealthy. This meant that there was not enough land available for cultivation. Both small-scale and big-scale farmers were affected greatly by a shortage of fertilizer. Even before 1916, the ordinary urban dweller began to protest against the authorities.

The January Strikes

The signs of the coming revolution began to emerge in the cold January 1917 with a general strikes that included thousands of railway workers. But strikes were not only about working conditions in the middle-class; they also had a political component. On Bloody Sunday, more than 100,000 workers and the public took part in a demonstration. The Russians weren't aware of the events that would become a full-blown anti-tsarist movement.

The January strikes went relatively peaceful, with a few clashes and disagreements with the authorities. The situation would only worsen over the coming days. The tsar had gone to St. Petersburg with the soldiers of the front lines and all calls for him to return fell on deaf ears. He ignored protests because of bad advice from the tsarina by mail. She pointed out that the poor protesters weren't much to do and would probably remain at home if the weather became worse.

February-The Revolution Takes Shape

It began with a scathing attack at the Duma. Mikhail Rodzianko among others, and prominent members in the assembly, began to express concern about the lack of interest by the tsar in the plights the striking workers. They suggested replacing the tsar's cabinet ministers, whom they considered incompetent.

The Duma, at the time, was only an advisory body and had few powers. But it was becoming increasingly hostile against the monarchy with more strikes over the major cities of the empire. Nicholas II was upset by the Duma's defiant nature and the criticisms of it. He ordered its abolition. This was ignored. It was also one the last mistakes he made as ruler over the Russian

Empire. The Duma's political parties would eventually join with the Petrograd Soviet, and plan his downfall.

Food rationing was imposed in major cities to address the shortage. However, it only made the already terrible situation worse. Panic buying caused an increase in food prices in the market and chaos as workers and others in cities rushed in order to stockpile food rations. This led to protests by women across the city demanding government action. Some protests were violent, with police clashing with protesters. This led to many fatalities due to the clamoring food. This was embarrassing to the monarchy. It also led to an increase the anger of the middle class, who felt trapped.

International Women's Day was on February 23, 1917. An enviable crowd of women numbered in the thousands joined by pro-revolutionary groups took over St. Petersburg's main street. They weren't there to observe International Women's Day. This was the largest ever anti-government protest in Tsar Nicholas's era. The banners were emblazoned with the message "DOWN TO THE TSAR", and carried signs.

More importantly, most of those troops that were supposed to be fighting the mobs joined the protesters and mutinied. One platoon was not ordered to fire at the protesters and instead chose to murder their commander and join them in protest. As they watched the demonstrations unfold, a large number of troops chose not to act.

The majority of the police officers and officials who maintained loyalty to tsar and used fire on crowds were arrested. The protest continued the following day with police stations and prisons being invaded. As the marauding crowd, empowered by the presence in their midst of armed mutineers, moved from establishment to establishment with the help of the tsar's symbols and statues, they were able to destroy the emblems and statues. The Russian Revolution officially began when the capital was under the control of the tsarists.

Nicholas II, who'd been away on military duties, finally tried to return the capital. But the ongoing railway strike hampered him more than anyone else. He couldn't travel to St. Petersburg due to a delay and was unable to reach the capital before the damage had been done. Petrograd Soviet as well as the Duma had already begun to plan his abdication. Ten days elapsed before the Women's Day protests ended. The 300-years-old Romanov rule would be over by those ten day. Russia's people rejoiced at the formation a new socialist and democratic administration. Could their wishes be fulfilled?

The Abdication the Tsar

The Duma had already made a deal with the Petrograd Soviet. They also had support from the top military commanders in the capital. Together they realized that Nicholas II had to be expelled from the picture to keep peace and quell the protests. To denounce Nicholas II and to change their allegiance, the military generals wrote letters.

Nicholas II didn't have to travel from Moscow to meet Duma officials. They met him in Pskov to pick up his train that had been delayed. The letters from the military generals presented to the tsar forced him to abdicate. Grand Duke Michael refused, but he did so until ordered by the assembly. The tsar, along with his family, were placed under house arrest before being executed. This marked both the end and beginning of the Romanov-era monarchy and a new, short-lived liberal government by the Mensheviks.

The Provisional Government

With the monarchy gone, the Duma members formed a provisional government which would temporarily take control until a democratic government was elected. It is much easier said then done. It would still be impossible to create a new constitution with Petrograd Soviet, the military-controlled Petrograd Soviet, being part the new government.

In the interim, the new provisional government had a number reforms in the pipeline. First was the abolition of the death sentence. The government also established a set of principles which would guide all its decisions.

Amnesty is granted for all political/religious and military revolts as well as offences relating to large scale farming. It is simple to understand the reasoning behind this principle. The majority of members and supporters of a provisional government were involved or influenced by one or more offenses. Petrograd Soviet military personnel were exempted for their role in the dissolution of the monarchy. Many top officials from the first committee of a provisional government were wealthy farmers and were members in good standing of the nobility.

Ensuring freedoms of the press and the right to unify, freedom speech, and the ability for military personnel to engage in politics. This is easy to grasp, particularly since the provisional Government was a military entity.

The abrogation of class, nationality, and religious discrimination. Russia was an amalgamation of diverse nationalities, tribes and cultures at that time. There were sharp social divisions due to class, wealth and origin. This principle was supposed to endear the government to the people.

The last principle concerned the preparation of plans for a referendum on a new constituent Assembly based in a democratic procedure and the drafting an amended constitution for a Russian state that will be subject to civil rule. The provisional government did not come to pass, much in the dismay and disappointment of the Russian people. Many historians actually blame the Russian Revolution, for failing to reach its goal of a democratically elect government.

It's important that you note that while there was a provisional government composed of moderate politicians, the Petrograd Soviet consisted of radical ex-revolutionary troops and soldiers. The provisional authority would soon be challenged by the Petrograd Soviet, which later passed orders restricting its powers. The Petrograd Soviet's repeated disputes with the provisional authorities lasted for months. Orders by the provisional authorities were often denied by the Petrograd Soviet and not considered seriously.

The involvement of the state in the World War II was a matter of concern to the Russian people. Contrary the popular belief, many ordinary Russians did not care as much about what was happening around Europe as they were their day to day lives as workers and farmers. The provisional government may also fall because of the tsar's decision in World War I to join the allied side.

The provisional government was expected by the Russian people to end the war in the world and make peace with Germany. That was what many political activists hoped for and what Lenin fought for since the war began. However, powerful voices within the government wanted Russia to support its allies in this war until its end. This group believed that the Russian Empire should remain a powerful and influential state on the international scene.

They also believed that Russia's future economic independence would be guaranteed if it remained in the war to its end. Russia would not have to rely solely on foreign aid and loans. Many government officials were also convinced that Russia was the loser and they would have more to gain if they tried to negotiate with the Germans.

This is why the provisional governments chose to keep a presence in war to the detriment and disappointment of the rest. Being at war meant those back home would continue to struggle from economic difficulties as most of the capital was being spent on military operations. Most of the ablebodied men and woman were active in the war, which left the farms to the rural peasants.

A leaked message to the allies that confirmed Russia's continued involvement during the war spurred riots across the capital. The brief honeymoon period for the provisional administration was about to end.

Chapter 4: The Return of Lenin
The New Revolution Is Here

After Russia's decision to continue World War I with its troops, the provisional governments was no longer considered a positive entity. A new wave of protests, as well as pressure from within government, forced Pavel Milyukov (the foreign minister) and Aleksandr Kerensky (the war minster) to resign. Aleksandr Kerensky stepped in and assumed the charge of the provisional administration.

Kerensky was socialist and pro war politician. Later, Kerensky would be confronted with the Bolsheviks. One of his first actions as leader was to launch an unsuccessful Austro Hungary offensive that saw thousands die. The Germans' inability and speed to react quickly to the situation and the underfed soldiers who led the unsuccessful offensive were major factors. This offensive was responsible for the deaths of more than 400,000 troops.

"There is no Russian Front. There is only one Allied front ."--Aleksandr Kerensky

Kerensky initially enjoyed popularity among the masses. He was able to stir up their emotions and convince them that Russia would be more powerful in the international arena if it continued its war efforts. British ambassador George Buchannan spoke highly of Kerensky, calling him a charismatic leader who was also a passionate patriot and whose leadership would make sure that the Russian nation didn't fall to anarchy.

Kerensky was the radical military general Lavr Kornilov who replaced Brusilov. Kerensky was always at loggerheads with Kornilov over many issues. Kerensky was forced by immense pressure from Lavr Kornilov to reintroduce capital punishment after this incident.

Many of the remaining soldiers fled their posts to join anti-government voices and joined them in the failed Austrohungarian offensive. Kornilov believed, as a punishment for deserters from the military, that the death penalty would deter soldiers joining forces with the Bolsheviks to overthrow their government.

The Kornilov Affair

Kornilov then sent troops to capital in an attempt to overthrow the government. Many historians believe that Kornilov was simply trying to show the Bolsheviks who were protesting against the provisional regime what they were against by ordering troops to the capital. Kerensky mistakenly believed that the move was a ploy to get help from Red Army, which was under the control and control of the Bolsheviks. Kornilov and thirty other military officers who stayed with him were arrested and sent to prison. The same group would later be the nucleus behind the dreaded White Army which went to war to overthrow Lenin's government.

Lenin had recently returned from exile and was working closely to the Bolshevik rebels who wanted Russia out the war. Lenin delivered an emotional speech to revolutionary proletariat upon his arrival at Finland Station. This speech would later be used as the basis for the "April Theses". Here's an excerpt from the April Theses in its original historical context.

Vladimir Ilyich Lenin, April Theses[1]

1) Our attitude towards this war, which, under the new [provisional] Government of Lvov and

Co. is unquestionably Russia's predatory imperialist War owing the capitalist nature and government, is not the slightest concession for "revolutionary Defencism"

The proletariat class conscious can agree to a revolutionary war, which would justify revolutionary defencism only on the condition that: (a. the power passes to the Proletariat and the most poorest sections of the peasants allied with the Proletariat; and (b. all annexes be renounced by word and in deed; and (c. a complete split be made in real time with all capitalist concerns.

Due to the obvious honesty of large parts of the revolutionary defencist masses who accept the war only because it is necessary and not for conquest, and due to the fact that the bourgeoisie are deceiving them, it becomes essential to explain their error to the masses, to explain capital's inseparable connection with the imperialist warfare, and to show that it is impossible, without overthrowing capitalism, to end the conflict by a true democratic peace. A peace that is not dictated by violence

The army at battle must organize the largest possible campaign in this direction.

2) Russia's current circumstances are unique because it is transitioning from the first phase of revolution, which, due to insufficient classes-consciousness and organization, gave power to the bourgeoisie, into its second stage. It must now give power to the proletariat (and the poorest parts of the peasants).

This transition is characterized, firstly, by a maximum in legally recognized rights (Russia now is the freest belligerent country in the entire world); secondly, by an absence of violence towards masses and, lastly, by their unreasoning belief in the government by capitalists who are the worst enemies and allies of peace and socialistism.

This particular situation requires us to be able adjust to the unique conditions of Party work among unimaginably large masses of proletarians that have just begun to awaken to political life.

3) There should be no support for the Provisional Government. The total falsity all of its promises should clearly be revealed, especially in relation

to the renunciation on annexations. An expose should replace the illegal, illusion-breeding, "demand" that this government be a government of capitalists.

4) Recognition of the fact that in most of the Soviets of Workers' Deputies our Party is in a minority, so far a small minority, as against a bloc of all the petty-bourgeois opportunist elements, from the Popular Socialists and the Socialist-Revolutionaries down to the Organizing Committee (Chkheidze, Tsereteli, etc. Steklov etc., who gave in to the bourgeoisie's influence and spread it among the proletariat.

The Soviets Of Workers' Deputies have to be explained to the masses as the only revolutionary form of government. Therefore, we must, so long as this government remains in power, present a persistent, patient, systematic, and persistent explanation for the errors of their tactics. It should also be tailored to the practical demands of the masses.

We continue to be critics and exposers of errors, even if we are in minority. But we also preach that it is necessary to transfer all state power over the Soviets for Workers' Deputies. So that the people may learn from their mistakes.

5). Not a Parliamentary Republic to Return to a Soviets of Workers' Republic would be a Retrograde Step, but a Republic of Soviets of Workers', Agriculture Laborers' and peasants' Deputies in the entire country, from Top to Bottom.

Abolitions of the police and the army.

All salaries for officials, including those who are elected and displaceable at anytime, cannot exceed the average wage of a competent employee.

6) The emphasis of the agrarian plan will shift to the Soviets for Agricultural Laborers' deputies.

Confiscation of all landed properties.

Nationalization of all lands of the country. Land to be disposed by the local Soviets Agricultural Laborers' and Peasants' Deputies. Organization of separate Soviets of Deputies of Poor Peasants. The creation of a model agricultural farm on each estate, ranging in size between 100 and 300 dessiatines, depending on the local conditions and the decision of the local bodies), which is under the control of Soviets Of Agricultural Laborers'Deputies.

7) The Union of all banks in the country to form a single national bank. The Soviet of Workers' Deputies is then given control.

8) It is not the immediate task of our Soviets to "introduce" socialism. However, it is necessary to bring social production to an end and distribute products immediately under the control to the Soviets.

9) Party tasks

(a. Immediate convocation at a Party congress

(b). Modification of Party Program, mainly

(1) About the question about imperialism and the conflict between imperialism

(2) Our attitude toward the state and demand for a "commune" state;

(3) The amendment of our outdated minimum program.

(c) Change of Party's Name

10. International.

We must act now to create an International of revolution, against the Centre and social-chauvinists.

Marxist ideologies were Lenin's favorite way to power and leadership. He had spent years studying the ideologies of Marxism and devised his own ideas on how rural and urban proletariats could liberate the state form the 300-year oppressive monarchy. Lenin desired a revolution since his youth, when he was a student. This desire was intensified after Alexander III executed Lenin's older brother, whom he had admired, as a child. The Ulyanov dynasty was always at war with the monarchy.

Some wonder if his return and eventual rise of power did not give the Russians an opportunity to realize the liberal democracy which they had long fought for. Lenin's return journey from exile in sealed carriage was shrouded within mystery. Kerensky was one of them. Kerensky also considered him a spy and traitor. It is believed that the Germans were the ones who enabled his entire journey. Kerensky later made public his condemnation of him as a traitor. Kerensky forced him into hiding during the July Days. After the Petrograd protests which rocked Petrograd, several Bolsheviks or soldiers were arrested.

But, the Bolsheviks managed to establish a strong military and political power by this point after they had been joined by Petrograd Soviet. Kornilov's attempted takeover of the capital saw his soldiers abandon him and cross the ranks to join the Bolsheviks. Now, the Bolsheviks had enough power that they could force Kerensky's government from power within days. The Petrograd Soviet freed most of the Bolsheviks held in jail and appointed Leon Trotsky to its chairman.

Lenin needed to return from Finland, where he had been hiding, after Moscow and Petrograd fell under the Bolsheviks. Lenin, upon his return, began work on a comprehensive program that would see Kerensky's provisional state overthrown.

Lenin desired the new revolution to lead to the total control by the Bolsheviks of Petrograd & Moscow. The central commission drafted a resolution calling upon the dissolution and demise of the provisional government by

September end. Lenin did all of this with his input. However, he still remained hiding for personal security.

Chapter 5: The October Revolution

Kerensky was viewed as a traitor by most military officers, whose popularity suffered greatly from the Kornilov investigation. The public's opinion of the charismatic leader, who was once thought to be the only one who could save Russia form anarchy, is at an all-time low. Lenin saw an opening to not only remove him but also to gain control over the entire government. Lenin forged a small front of military leaders from Petrograd to form the MRC (Military Revolutionary Front), that would lead October's uprisings. He directed the troops to occupy the Winter Palace, October 25th.

The Storming of the Winter Palace.

Nighttime storming in the Winter Palace was the first sign of the Lenin led October Revolution. It was where the provisional government held its meetings. Kerensky was arrested with all of his ministers. Mensheviks & the Socialist Revolutionary Party staged their own walkout. The Bolsheviks seized the opportunity to retake the congress in the form of a walkout. Lenin was able to stage a bloodless coup, and take over the government. He would sign later the Treaty of Brest-Litovsk in agreement with the Germans and then move his base to Moscow's Kremlin.

Lenin's rise created a communist superpower - the Soviet Union. The October decree, a promise made by the Bolshevik government, was read out by Lenin a day after the capture of Petrograd. The decree asked all Russians to contact their leaders and begin negotiations to secure a peaceful future. The decree that formed a soviet state was signed by Vladimir Ulyanov (Lenin), chairman of the group, and all its ministers. It was announced at the Second All Soviet Congress of Soldiers' and Workers' Deputies' Soviets.

The 1917 Decree to Form a Soviet Govt[2]

The All-Russia Congress of Soviets of Soldiers, Workers, and Peasants Deputies resolves

To create a provisional workers' or peasants' administration, to be known by the Council of People's Commissars. This government will govern the country up to the Constituent Assembly.

Each branch of state activities is managed by individual commissions. Commission members are accountable for ensuring the Congress's fulfillment of its program. They shall also work closely with mass organizations that include sailors, fishermen, soldiers, office workers, and other employees.

The Council of People's Commissars holds the power to give government authority.

The All-Russia Congress of Soviets of Workers, Peasants and Soldiers Deputies and the Central Executive Committee hold control of the People's Commissars' operations and the right of replacement.

The Council of People's Commissars has been constituted as follows at the moment:

* Chairman, Council--Vladimir Ulyanov.

* People's Commissar at the Interior-Rykov

* Agriculture--Milyutin.

* Labor--Shlyapnikov.

* Army Affairs and Navy Affairs - a committee made up of Dybenko Krylenko Dybenko, Ovseyenko Krylenko.

* Commerce and Industry -- Nogin

* Education--Lunacharsky.

* Finance--Stepanov.

* Foreign Affairs--Bronstein.

* Justice--Oppokov.

* Food--Tedorovich.

* Posts and Telegraphs - Avilov

* Chairman for Nationalities--Jugashvili.

* The People's Commissar of Railways' office is temporarily unoccupied.

To address the Russian Empire's historical land problems, the Bolshevik government made these land decrees.

Bolshevik Land Decree on Land of 1917[3]

1. Without compensation, leased proprietorship [ownership] ceases immediately.

2. The landed estates together with all crown-, monastery-, and Church lands, their livestock, implements buildings, etc., will be available to the Soviets Of Peasants'Deputies and land

committees until the Constituent Assembly convenes.

3. All damage to confiscated goods, which are now the property of the entire people, is deemed a grave crime that will be punished in revolutionary courts.

4. The Soviets' Peasants' Deputies shall take all necessary precautions to ensure that there is no infringement of law during confiscation. These measures include determining the size and nature of any estates and the estates most likely to be confiscated, establishing exact inventories of all confiscated property, protecting all agricultural enterprises and all buildings, tools, and produce stores.

Chapter 6: Early History (800-1200).

Scholars are generally unanimous in agreeing that Russia today was established in 882 A.D. through the establishment of the Kievan Russ' kingdom. Belarusians can be traced back to their ancestors through the East Slavs. This confederation lasted for around 358years. The Rurik dynasty, for the most, ruled the kingdom.

Oleg von Novgorod, who ruled for 33 years between 882-912 and his death, was not the only historical figure to rule the Rus'.

Kievan Russ' under Prince Oleg's Regiment

Oleg's history is so complex that it's difficult to locate a reliable source. However, it is known that he seized Kiev from Askold, his brother and put the foundation for the Rus'. Kiev will be the centre of what is to become the Rus' vast kingdom. Another theory says that the Kievan Rus existed before the Rus's creation and was ruled at the time by Rurik the Prince of Ladoga. Oleg, however, might have inherited it.

Oleg, who was so recklessly bold that he launched an assault on Constantinople, seems to have had a rather condescending personality. This allowed for trade to be established between the two countries. Oleg and the period in which he ruled are different from what is reported in various chronicles. The facts don't always fit the historical narratives.

We know that Oleg died in 912. However, the circumstances are at best vague. Oleg might have died of snakebite. However, since this piece of information is fictional (Pushkin's The Song of the Wise Oleg), it seems less likely.

Oleg reigned over the land and helped it prosper by bringing many cities to it. He is also credited for helping to make the Kievan Rus' reach their commercial peak by developing trades using furs.

Oleg's 912 death was followed by another Varangian prince (from the Rurik Dynasty) who ruled over the flourishing Kievan Rus'. His name, Igor of Kiev or Igor Igor 1, was as mysterious and mysterious as his predecessor.

The Russe under Igor Kiev's Reign

In 914 Oleg died, Igor from Kiev became ruler. According to Oleg, Rurik's father and - many believe – the first ruler of Kievan Rus', Igor's care was taken by Oleg. The Primary Chronicle, the oldest information source on the history the Rus''s history, is Igor's story. As you can see there are not many details about the Rus''s history that have been etched into stone.

It is not known much about the Rus' under Igor's rule. It isn't even known much about his life. Historians are confused. It is claimed that Igor never ruled as long as history accepts (33 years). However, we know that Oleg followed Igor's lead and attacked Constantinople twice. This led to another benefit treaty between these two empires.

Drevlians claimed that Igor was killed. This tribe is where he received his tribute. This occurred in 945 and ended Igor's reign over the Kievan Rus'. A Byzantine chronicler says that Igor was tied with two bent trees. He was then cut in half by straightening the trees.

Sviatoslav I, between 945 to 972, and Yaropolk III (between 932-962) ruled the Kievan Rus'. Vladimir The Great, who promoted Christianization in the Kievan Rus''s history, is the next big moment.

Vladimir the Great's Triumph over the KievanRus''

Vladimir the great, Yaropolk's son, ruled for 35 years in the Rus', between 980-1015. When he died at the ripe old age of 57. He expanded the Rus' empire by conquering other tribes and forming new colonies pertaining directly to the Rus'. In 981, the territory which today includes southeastern Poland as well as the west part of Ukraine was conquered by him. One can see that it had only been a year since he ascended to the throne. Then he expanded the Rus'. He conquered Sudovians, 983, and one-year later, he destroyed the Radimichs. The Kievan's Rus was a hasty development, but Vladimir was far more than a ruthless and blood-thirsty leader. He was an extraordinarily charitable person and this is probably why he received the sainthood of both the Eastern Orthodox Church as well as the Roman Catholic.

Before his reign, the Rus' only practiced paganism. Vladimir was a pagan for the majority of his life. In fact, Perun was probably worshiped at that time. But all this was about to change.

Vladimir is, in actuality, one the most important people in the history the Kievan Rus'.

It's not easy to Christianize an ancient pagan kingdom. It is not difficult to see that anyone who attempted this feat was met with resistance more than praise. The Christianizations of the Kievan Rus' was a major impact on the Rus', and the entire history of Russia. First of all Christianity was a more "educated", so to speak. This cultural infiltration helped to create Slavic literature. We know today how essential Slavic religious texts can be. Those texts would have never existed if Vladimir did not Christianize pagan Kievan Rus'.

He became the ruler and chief of the Kievan Rus' through the killing of his brother Yaropolk. His conquering efforts were assisted by the Norse soldiers of Haakon Sigurdsonn. These warriors ruled Norway in 975-995. Through him, the Kievan Rus' reached economic success as he established many trades between Greece and Arabia. Needless to state, the kingdom flourished. Yaroslav I, his successor, will continue this trend.

It is important to note that Vladimir was a humane man, but he also waged war against his son for not paying him enough respect. Vladimir did not live to see the day when he could take action. He became sick and then died. Sviatopolk of the Accursed occupied the throne for four years after Vladimir's passing. Fratricide, which was common at the time, was not uncommon. Fratricide was, evidently, a normal part of daily living. Vladimir, later sainted & praised, actually killed his brother for the chance to ascend to throne. Yaroslavthe Wise does not seem to be an exception to this very odd rule.

He was succeeded by his brother Sviatopolk a Cursed who had seized Kiev and killed 3 of his siblings (disputable). Between 1019-1054 Yaroslavthe Wise ruled over all the Rus'. His reign was the moment the Kievan Rus' became an absolute military power and cultural power.

Yaroslav's most loved implementation was the Russkaya Pravda. This became the Kievan Rus' code of law and served as a template for other codes as they were built over the years. Yaroslav also tried to follow in his predecessors' footsteps by trying to conquer Constantinople. Although he wasn't successful, there was still an upside to all of it: a tie towards the Byzantine Emperor. Vladimir Yaroslavich, Yaroslav's son, was made the Byzantine monarch. This led both to improved relations and politics with the Empire.

Yaroslav's city-building prowess can still be seen in Poland, Russia Ukraine and Estonia. Even though Kievan Rus' had become an icon of culture, it was already headed for monumental ruin.

The Last Prince Of Kievan Rus' And the Decline of the Empire

Between 1054 when Yaroslav was killed and 1236 when Michael of Chernigov took power, there were many rulers in the kingdom. Six princes or more were responsible for the Kingdom during this 182-year-long period.

(Saint Michael of Chernigov) is the last individual that we are interested in. He was the last ruler over the wealthy and thriving Kievan Rus' just before the collapse. The Rus' were ruled by him in two sessions. While his reign was short-lived in both instances he was as potent as any of his predecessors.

He just happened be in power at a time of turmoil, which hinted at the imminent destruction of the empire. Constantinople's collapse was right around the corner. This cut off the Byzantium's commercial trades. This wasn't what caused the decline of the Kievan Rus'. But there was something else: the invasion and destruction of the Mongols just as they had become a scourge of Europe.

They were unstoppable. They took control of several Rus' cities, and between 1223- 1240, there were numerous waves of invasions by the Mongolians that completely destroyed the Kievan Rus'. Michael of Chernigov tried desperately to unite the princes in the principalities, Rus', to withstand this impending disaster. But his efforts were unsuccessful. He refused to agree to peace with Batu Kahn and even killed his messengers.

Due to his limited military strength, he sought asylum from Hungary. After a brief period, he was expelled in the hands of Bela IV, then-king and queen of Hungary. It is important that it should be noted that many Mongols allowed their princes to keep both their statuses or their principalities. However, this came at a cost: they had to kneel before the Mongolian leader and accept the Mongolian idols.

Michael of Chernigov is the last prince of Kievan' Rus'. His refusal to worship idols led to Batu Khan ordering his execution. He was eventually made a martyr. He was also the only Kievan ruler to not bow before the Mongols. Today, Michael Chernigov is one among the Russian people's patron saints.

Mongolian Domination

Russia fell into the Mongolian domination after he died. To inoculate against the Golden Horde's influence, the Russians fought a number of battles with Tatars. Mstislavich's reign of the moribund Rus' ended with the Battle of the Kalka River. The Mongols were already at war in the neighboring countries and showed no sign of slowing down. The Mongol hordes converged on the Dniester in a warning sign that they were about to invade the Rus'. Mstislav refused to remain passive. Contrariwise he formed an alliance to the Rus' with the other princes, in an effort severing the Mongolian threat.

The Kievan Rus' army began to march towards the Dniester. In the beginning, the Mongolians accepted the benefit and sent messengers to clarify that they weren't interested sacking the kingdom. They had a bone for the Cumans. Mstislav II of Kiev was not pleased with this and slew Jebe, Genghis Kan's general. This started the war. The Kievan Rus' armies thought that they were retreating. However, the Mongolians didn't retreat; they were just acting as such in order for the Rus to take their armies to the Kalka River.

Mstislav Mstislavich's army, along with other princes he had fought, was a major factor in the downfall of the Mongols. Confusion, the absence a true leader of the Kievan Rus' armies (each of Mstislav's princes engaged did whatever he desired) and the stampeding Cumans (on the way to retreat) all contributed to the bloody defeat the Kievan army along the Kalka River.

Eventually, however, some elements of the Kievan force managed to escape the chaos. Mstislav Mstislavich, for instance, was able to escape. Some of them fled towards Ploscanea to be killed. Only half the princes summoned and saved by Mstislav was able to save their own lives. Mstislav fled for Torchesk and died five years later. The Mongolian army was constantly under attack after the defeat. Their superior military prowess as well their sheer number were insurmountable. Genghis Khan, the invader Mongols, was defeated.

In 1237, Batu Khan (and Subutai) invaded the kingdom and brought with them a force more than 100.000 Mongols. The result was decades of subjugation in Mongol rule and very little advancement. It was not all bad. The Golden Horde was also a positive force.

1237 is a key year in the Kievan Rus' history, and later in the Russian history. It marks a beginning of the occupation and rule of the Golden Horde. The Mongols seized the Kievan Rus' principalities and demolished them. Those remaining functional were made into the Mongolian empire's appanages. Despite this being a sad chapter in Russian History, some historians argue that without Mongolian rule, the Tsardom could not have happened.

The Mongols introduced many reforms to the ex-Kiew Rus'. Some of their principalities even flourished while they were in power. Because the Mongols were considered a godly punishment, a dual tax system and greater power for the Orthodox church over the people was created. Moscow saw an economic boom, which enabled the establishment of the future tsardom. Additionally, power was centralized (which is not necessarily a good thing). The Mongolian rule had two major disadvantages. One, it prevented Russia from making significant intellectual progress while it was still in power and two, it kept Russia isolated for 250 years.

According to some researchers the Mongolian influence was responsible for Russian's language. Russian researchers split into two camps. One side believes that Mongolian rule didn't have any effect on Russia and denies its influence. The other, however, believes that Mongolian influence is enormous. The truth is probably somewhere in between.

The Golden Horde continued to be in power until 1380, when Dmitri von Moscow made the first attempt against the Mongols dominance. His battle against Mamai Khan is remembered as the Battle Of Kulikovo. This war is a key point in Russian historical history. It is the first major retaliation for the Russians against Mongolian dominance. Tokhtamysh was the Khan conquered Moscow in 1382 and maintained their sovereignty despite all this. But this was not an act of tragedy. No more. Dmitri was victorious, and it proved that the Russian people are capable of getting rid Tatar pest.

The conflict flared up in Russia's deepest bowels. The Mongols' dominance over the Russians made them sicker and there were many signs that signaled the final rebellion. In 1480, the Great Stand on Ugra River became the most important battle between Mongols und Russians. This defeat of their influence was decisive. This was the pivotal conflict that determined the fate and destiny of the Russian nation. Ivan III led the Great Duchy of Moscow which was the blueprint for the Tsardom. He was to confront the Great Horde led by Akhmat Kan.

Russians' victory was based on their possession of firearms, and their numbers. The "battle," however, was not really "battle". The conflict did not escalate into a physical battle. Akhmat Khon waited for reinforcements, but they didn't come. He knew he would be defeated by the Russian forces.

This conflict opened the way to Russia's Tsardom and thus the Russian Empire. Even though it might seem that the Mongols were restored by the Tsardom (which one may believe), this is not true. It began with blood and ended in exactly the same way. Let's examine the next 250 years of Mongolian rule.

Early Russian History, Misconception

While we attempt to preserve historical facts as accurately and as accurately possible, there are always people who hear it wrong and spread the bad news. Here are some misinformations you may have seen.

* Russians are serious people. They have never laughed and lack humor. This is actually the complete opposite. Russians have a strong sense of humor and are similar in their outlook to outgoing Americans.

* They believe Ukraine begins with the Kievan Rus Empire. This is however not true. While the Kievan Rus certainly played a role shaping Ukraine today's history, it wasn't with Russia. It was much earlier than the time Russia was formed.

Unusual Facts That You May Not Be Aware Of

* The Kievan Rus' explains why Russians (and Ukrainians) share the same blood. Even after hundreds of years, they still can trace their heritage back to the inhabitants of this kingdom.

* At the time that the Rus' existed, the Mongols ruled the globe. The sight of Mongolian riders riding across a field was a sign of infliction.

* The Kievan Rus' existed between 882-988 and was a pagan state.

If the Choice Was Yours

History is fascinating for its educational potential. Let's see how you would react to certain circumstances.

* If Vladimir The Great had been alive, would he have Christianized the Kievan Rus?

* Michael Chernigov refused not to bow before Batu Khan and his idols. If you were Michael of Chernigov, would you have bowed your head in order to save you life or would it have been as an expression of your faith?

* Would Ivan III have had the courage, if he were Ivan III to challenge Tatar dominance and win the match on The Great Stand at the Ugra River.

Questionnaire

1. How many years did it take for the KievanRus to die?

2. How long was Oleg de Novgorod's reign

3. Who Christiansized the KievanRus'

4. What dynasty does the KievanRus have in common?

Chapter 7: Tsardom In Russia (1500-1500).

The Russian Tsardom lasted 174 Years, that is, between 1547 and 1721. Russia grew tremendously over the course of this period. We will soon see why it is so difficult to control such a huge territory.

The Tsardom and Revolution of Russia are without doubt the most important stages in Russian history, apart from the Soviet Union. It began with bloodshed. It ended in no other way. The country's large size played a significant role in the upheavals and chaos that characterize the Tsardom. All of the subsequent rulers assumed the same rank when he died in 1584. The Tsardom was also the moment that Russia became the common name for the state. In the past, Russia was known simply as Russia, Russia, or Moscovia. The latter was used in a form of defense, to distinguish between the two parts which made up the Kievan Rus' - the Muscovite country and its Lithuanian counterpart.

The Russian rulers sought to ascend to the highest echelon by giving them the title of "Tsar." Mongolians had the name of Khan, which was an honorable and respected title. The Byzantine

Empire had "Emperor" and "Prince." These two sound so much better than these. So, a new title was needed. Ivan the Terrible, by taking the title "Tsar", elevated himself to the exact same place in the hierarchy of the Khans as the Emperors.

All these things would mean that the title would come with a lot of responsibility. It was often more of an evil than a blessing. Many of the Tsars used to slaughter their subjects to calm down this artificial sense of superiority. When one examines the history of Russia's Tsardom, and the Tsars who marched through it from Ivanthe Terrible onwards, one can see just how "divine," this Tsar was. To put it briefly, the Tsar became a God among people. Gods, as history has shown, can be brutal.

The Tsardom also signified the change from the Rurik Dynasty to one of the Romanovs. This was not achieved without violence. Furthermore, relations between Russia and Poland and Grand Duchy of Lithuania began to deteriorate. This resulted in years of conflict which didn't help Tsar Nicholas II.

There are six distinct stages of Russian historical development: Grand Duchy of Moscow (1283-

1547), Russia's Crown (1547-1721), Russia's Imperial (1721-1721), Russia's Russian Empire (1721-1717), Russia's Russian Republic (1917), Russia's Soviet Union (1822-1991), and then the period between its dissolution and the present.

The Grand Duchy of Moscow, briefly covered in the preceding chapter, ended when Ivanthe Terrible was elected to power. We will also discuss the various stages but for the time being, we will focus on the Tsardom itself and its implications.

Ivan the Terrible- the First tsar

Ivan The Terrible is a vivid portrayal of Russia's historical past. He ruled between 1547 & 1584 for 37 years. He had a very dyadic personality, it seems. He had a great diplomacy and was extremely intelligent. He was also proficient in arts, literature, and trades. On the other, he was very mentally challenged. He often suffered from depression and paranoia. Sometimes he even became violent. As he grew old, his mental illnesses continued to degenerate. His family, Russia, and the Russian people were the most frequent targets.

Ivan successfully completed Russia's transition to a modern, stable state. Russia began to attain its enormous size during his reign. This however did not come at a cheap price. No. The state was on the verge of an economic crash that would trigger the Time of Troubles, one of Russia's darkest periods in history. Russia's money was rapidly effected by his brutal expansion wars.

Russians had a difficult time during the Tsardom. Ivan was unable to lead because of his mental instability. It's safe enough to say that his madness reached a peak with the creation Oprichnina. A division between the Oprichnina as the ultimate power and those in the rest. A chain of traitors made the Tsar paranoid skyrocket and the aristocrats/nobility suddenly became his worst enemy.

Oprichnina policy which gave him absolute power led to gratuitous bloodshed. Ivan began massacring innocent people (not poor nor wealthy) with the Oprichnina policy. To shorten the story, he could never be held responsible by anyone, changing the status from "Tsar", to something very similar, "God."

Ivan's personal guard the Oprichniki conducted the massacres. They were paid with privileges. lands. and their lives. Novgorod fell to ashes during the plague of 1570.

As a direct consequence of Oprichnina's actions, 12,000 people were murdered 1570 in what would become the Massacre of Novgorod. The Massacre of Novgorod is the most egregious evidence of the Tsar's dangerous madness. Some historians say that Ivan the Terrible was the one who initiated the attack, although this is not definitive. The psychological slippage of Ivan the Terrible was caused by a number of factors. It is believed that the boyars wanted Poland to take over the city. This was probably the final straw for a mentally unstable Tsar. Ivan executed every thing he saw fit, following a "Better to prevent than cure" ideology. Even though Russia did expand under his reign it is not an acceptable historical stage.

Although Ivan the Terrible is credited with many trades and the founding of Russia's premier publishing house, these achievements pale when compared to the more desirable ones. The truth is that violence can breed violence. Ivan was only a part of what was going to happen to Russia, and the way it would change its character. All of the consequences of Ivan the Tsar's deeds and Ivan the Tsardom can be summarised in the words the Strugatsky brother: it is "hard not to be god."

Even though Ivan was still alive, famine was already causing havoc. But it wasn't famine as such that it was alarming. Feodor I was the new Russian leader, eager to put an end to the state that had been left without money and food by his father.

The Time of Trouble

Feodor, Ivan's son, was not as competent as his father in ruling. While "reigned", is the wrong word here, he was the ruler of the Tsardom from 1504 to 1598. He was not an expert in politics, and he did not wish to be familiar with the tasks and duties that a Tsar would have.

According to some sources, he was mentally unstable like his father. The situation could have turned out differently if Ivan Ivanovich didn't kill his son Ivan Ivanovich. Some sources suggest that Ivan Ivanovich is a talented young man. On some level, he might have outperformed his father.

This is why it was not Feodor's reign, but Boris Godunov who governed the state behind the scenes as regent. Boris Godunov, Feodor I's administrator and political abilities were very poor. Boris Godunov was therefore the de facto ruler. Boris, on other hand, was a much greater fit for the throne. It was his that Feodor lost. His reign began in 1598 on the 21stof February. Boris Godunov exemplified the role of a regent. His policy was always one of diplomacy and he avoided any wars.

His primary concern was education, and his administration. Russians had access to education for the first-ever time under his leadership, with most of it being provided by foreign professors. Some of those who were considered capable enough were sent to foreign countries to acquire an even greater degree of intelligence.

Boris Godunov's ability to control the weather was one thing that he couldn't do. Extremely low temperatures frost the crops, leading the to the Russian famine. It lasted two years, from 1601 to 1603. There are estimates that about 2 million Russians were killed in the span of two years. There have been many other famines over

Russian history. However, none were so severe and had such genocidal-like characteristics.

Both Ivan and Feodor came from the Rurikid family. Feodor died in childlessness, closing the Rurikid coffin. The Godunov dynasty was born with Boris Godunov. Unfortunately, this event brought on the Time of Troubles.

The Time of Troubles (or the Time of Troubles) was a time of severe famine, during which 2 million people died. It was between 1598-1613. The Godunov-dynasty was then replaced by the Romanov. Although it is inefficient and dysfunctional, the former will lead for 300+ years. Russia plunged into chaos during 15 years of rebellions and civil warfare and was almost insolvent.

Boris Godunov's nephew, Feodor II Russia's son, assumed the throne but he only ruled for two or three months. His mother was also assassinated on June 20, 1605.

The Time of Troubles escalated. The mysterious figure known as the "False Dmitri", who reigned for approximately a year, did little to improve the situation. He formed an army to retake the throne. His reign wasn't peaceful. His ultimate goal appeared to be war with the Ottoman Empire. Godunov did not continue his social and educational reforms. He was ultimately executed at the Kremlin.

As if political, social, and economic disequilibrium didn't suffice during the Time of Troubles there was also a drastic shift in climate that made it impossible for peoples to cultivate anything. Needless to state, food costs rose. This only added to the other problems that plagued Russia's Tsardom. It also increased them and helped accelerate the country's fall.

All these cataclysmic happenings stopped once Mikhail Romanov crowned tsar, in 1613. However, the crisis might have continued if Poland did not intervene in 1609; however, the pandemonium passed once the Russians realized they wanted to get rid of the Poles from Kremlin. However, a peace agreement with Poland was reached soon after. It didn't last for long.

Between 1598-1613, 15 years of the Time of Troubles was elapsed. The economy and governance suffered serious blows in this period.

But, the Tsardom might have survived longer if it hadn't been for this agitated time.

The End to Russia's Tsardom

Russia faced many challenges even after The Time of Troubles. Rebellions continued to be ignited whenever they had the chance. The Church was almost ripped apart during the Schism (1667), when relations between Russia, Poland and Russia became so bad that the "13 years of war" was begun (1654-1667).

Russia's isolation was the greatest problem in those days. It was not in line the other countries' systems. To a certain extent it was Europe's outcast. Yes, it was a massive military power, however, it was mostly a local power. The situation remained the same until Peter the Great created his "Grandembassy" in 1697. "Tsar" was still in circulation up until Nicholas' execution.

Russia won a lot more territories after the Russo–Polish conflict ended. This marked the end for the Tsardom (and the beginning and end of Russia's Empire). Russia was growing too large for it to be considered "Tsardom." But, on the other side, the Tsarist autocracy began to decline so quickly, in spite of the new Emperor. Additionally, the "Tsardom", was associated with too many historical afflictions. The 17th-century was very much in what modernity called "modernity." Tsardom could not be had anymore. The Byzantine Empire, along with the Mongolian Khanates, was no more. This was how "Tsardom", a reference to past times, really came across.

Radical change was once again necessary. The Russian people had never been used to the fact that this change was for the best. Many of the wrongdoings by the Tsardom were corrected by the newly-formed Imperial. Russia became an Empire to unite with its European neighbors. It was positively affected in all areas of education, politics and the management of society. Russians were not so impressionable. They needed a visionary leader who could show them how to make the most of their potential and explain why.

Russia's most violent historical moment is the Tsardom. The state has been to hell several times in its history, and that was just in 174 years. It was subjected the madness of Tsars, the incompetence and rebellions of his son, famines, droughts, wars as well civil wars.

The Russian history ended with the death of the Tsar in 1721. Peter the Great was burdened by the fact that Russia, Sweden, Poland, Poland and Poland were preparing to unleash their Great Northern War, which lasted 21+ years. Peter The Great had the opportunity to prove his strength and wit in this war.

He is undoubtedly the most revered and honorable Russian historian. He was able to make an empire out of the ashes & mud left by Tsardom. It was not an easy task. Not even by a very long shot. His reign was one of Russia's greatest and most successful. He healed many wounds, which seemed insurmountable. The most important thing is that he inspired future rulers in Russia to improve the Empire by introducing many cultural and educational reforms.

The Tsardom saw the end of the mythical tsar who was considered a godly person among mortals. Russia had been an incontestable country with an unquenchable thirst to survive. However, it is only after it becomes an Empire does it become one of Europe's greatest powers. The Russian Empire, or the Russian Empire as it was known, is our next chapter. Although it is not entirely free from pressures, it was much better than Russia's Tsardom.

A Misperception of the Tsardom

* Alexis the second Romanov-Tsar of Russia was a gentle, mild-tempered ruler. While it may have been true, it was only for show. Alexis, in fact, was the kinda person who would whip a revolting peasant with an iron and torture him while he was still breathing.

* Russia's true ruler, Tsar Nicholas, wasn't the one. Many believe that Nicholas was advised to lead the country by Rasputin. However most of Rasputin's ideas weren't applicable to Nicholas. Even though he provided a lot advice, it is difficult to say that Rasputin ruled the country.

Fascinating Facts About Russia's Tsardom

* During Tsardom Philoteus (head of the Yelizarov Convent) claimed that Russia was 3rd Rome. This hinted at the formation Russia's Empire.

* Ivanthe Terrible was just three years when he was made Grand Prince in Moscow.

* There were three False dmitries who pretended to be the throne. Not just one.

If you had the option

During this period of turbulent Russian history, many rulers made less-efficient decisions. However, would you have done things differently?

* If Boris Godunov had been alive, what would have you done to reduce or even reverse the negative effects of the Time of Troubles.

* Feodor I (Russia) accepted the leadership. However, he knew that he was not fit to govern, both politically and mentally. Would you make the same decision or step down?

* Assume you were one among the Oprichniki. Would you have followed the orders and killed innocent civilians?

Questionnaire:

1. How many years was Russia's Tsardom in existence?

2. What was Ivan's name?

3. Who was Feodor the prince regent in his reign?

4. Who and why did Rurikid dynasty fall?

Chapter 8: Imperial Russia, 1800 - 1900

The Russian Empire precedes its successor, the Russian Republic. The Empire was established 1721 and existed until 1917. As we might have stated in the previous section the Empire was massive and Peter, the Great, played a significant part in making it happen. The 17th-century marks the beginnings of the Russian Empire's story.

When you think about it, even Ivan IV's reign was not the Russian Empire. It's only that the denomination was different. The country had enough territory for it to be declared an empire. But it would be much more difficult to grasp the meaning of "Tsardom" or "Empire". Each name has a different meaning. The former refers to the end of the world, the latter to profound reform across the entire spectrum.

The fall of four major European/Asian imperial powers is what led to the rise of Russia. Russia was able, thanks to Russia's own contributions to getting rid these powers apart, to climb to the top of the list by dissolving them.

Russia as an empire should be discussed in the context of two important personalities: Peter the Great, and Ivan III.

Setting the Blueprint for the Empire

Russia was three times as big when Ivan III reigned as the successor to Vasili I of Russia. Russia's independence from the Great Horde, which has exerted a powerful control over it ever since the Mongols pillaged its land, was owned by Ivan III. The Great Stand of the Ugra River, which took place in 1480, is considered the moment that brought about this event.

Ivan III, unlike other rulers sought to end the Tatars' tributes. This resulted in the conflict. The Tatars were numerically overwhelmed and they left without engaging with any kind of combat. Casimir IV the Polish King promised military support but never delivered. Russia was split up into three distinct parts prior to Ivan's reign: Moscow and Tver.

They were constantly at war because each region had a different legislature. IvanIII made demarches that united the lands and established the foundation for the future Empire. Ivan III used force to conquer any lands not under his command. Russia was the one piece of land that Ivan III had managed to successfully incorporate. It was clear that there was only one law which all and everyone could abide to. If Ivan IV had not done so, it would have made the task of the Emperors much more difficult. Russia would not be an Empire, if not for a very long time.

Vasili III, his son after his death, completed the annexation and integration of the Muscovite-ruled districts. Russia then experienced a period full of difficulties, with both incompetent but witty rulers and impostors. Peter the Great, the ascending ruler of Russia's Empire, is the next important moment in its history.

Peter the great - Fleshing the Empire

The Empire had existed under the same inefficient, medieval system prior to Peter's reign. But, Europe was already making substantial progress. Peter was educated by many famous scholars of his time. He had a fast wit and a desire change the world for the better.

To take over Russia and implement his reforms, it was necessary for him to wait until Natalya Naryshkina, the mother of his son, died. He was made the sovereign in 1696. Then he began modernizing the country. Despite opposition, he was able to create the foundations for a Russian naval facility. This was to transform Russia from a fearful maritime power.

Even during his reign the Ottoman Empire was alive and well. This empire had also parasitized large parts of Europe. Peter understood that Russia's modernization could not proceed without ending the Ottoman threat. He attempted to make an alliance with the Ottomans, but this was mostly in vain. He spent a year and half wandering through Europe looking for help.

His journeys were not entirely futile. He came to admire the Western systems in Europe. These systems were a catalyst for his perseverance in getting Russia to the forefront of progress.

He returned to Sweden with the first goal of retaking the Baltic Sea from Swedes. He waged war. This led to what is now known as the Great Northern War (1700-1721). The victory was decisive and proved to everyone that Russia was not as weak in warfare as previously thought. He was officially named Emperor on 22nd October 1721.

This is when he made a series, mostly in education and politics, of changes to Russia (the Russian Empire). He expanded Russian territory by defeating the Safavid Emperor (in Russo-Persian War), annexing six of its provincials to the Empire. He was instrumental in westernizing Russia and modernizing the Army. He turned Russia from a poor, insecure, medieval country to a formidable European power.

Between 1682-1721 Peter the Great was Russia's Emperor. It was during this period that the Tsardom fell and Imperial Russia emerged in all its glory.

The Romanov family, to which Peter belonged, was going to end soon. Catherine I of Russia, Peter II of Russia's nephew and wife, succeeded him after his death. Peter II died young and left no children. It ended the Romanov Dynasty.

Peter II was more attracted to the title of "Emperor" as than he was to actually fulfilling his duties. Russia did indeed not go backwards. His 3-year reign proved to be not very significant. While the economy was unstable, there were not many catastrophic events. Like other royal children before he, he was drawn to entertainment because he had not been able to have the experience needed by an Emperor to oversee an Empire stretching as far as the eye can see. 14-years old is definitely not "programmed" for much.

After his death the Empire was led 4 times: Anna of Russia (1730-1740), Ivan VI (1740-1741), Elizabeth Petrovna (1762) and Peter III (1762). Each of them had different levels of effectiveness in their leadership. The Empress Catherine, an intellectual and diaphanous belligerent, was the next in line. She brought the Empire on track and continued to develop it on all levels.

Russia under Catherine the Great (1762-1796).

Although all the emperors of Russia who succeeded Peter II were physically fit, Catherine the Great, who was elected to power in 1762 proved more resilient and skillful than any other empresses and emperors. She was an avid follower of Peter, the Great, and his attempts to westernize Russia. It is because of this that she continued to push the Empire through endless reforms. It was under her reign that the Russian Empire reached its undisputed peak.

Catherine the Great has another interesting fact. She was the last person to strike the Ottoman Empire in the wars waged between the Russians (Turkish) and the Russians. She was, apparently, far from being an helpless woman. She actually had very strong military and strategic insights. While she carried out many reforms on Russian soil, she also dealt directly with war. The Turkish suffered some the worst losses in the Russo-Turkish War between 1768-1774.

A few years later in 1783 was the annexe of Crimea. Between 1787 and 1792, the Turkish started retaliations in context of the second Russo–Turkish war. They were trying to retake Crimea. They failed miserably again. Catherine the Great continued on. In 1796, Catherine the Great declared war on Persia. This is another inconclusive war of Russian history. Because Catherine the Great died, it didn't escalate.

To some degree education played a larger role in Russia's expansion than conquests. Peter the Great had made compulsory schooling compulsory for the nobility as well as the officials and children. He was Enlightened, even though the Age of Enlightenment began at the

18thcentury. Catherine was also given this role, and she did so with a determined determination to infuse Russia of proper education and values.

Catherine's respect and admiration of Peter and the system and type of knowledge he represented drove her to increase her focus on education. Her most significant accomplishment was the founding of several schools, including Smolny Institute which provided education to women. It was the first such institution in Europe. She also founded the Hermitage Musem, the Great Theater and built new cities.

Catherine the Great ruled and the Empire grew to unimaginable heights. Although she seems like a simple woman, her foreign relations policy often included aggressive wars. This helped to grow the Russian Empire. She was just as much a warrior than she was an enlightened Empress. Paul I, her son who relied upon diplomacy, was not able to assume this divide temper policy.

The Reign of Paul i

Paul I ruled over Persia for five more years. He was always against his mother's will. He directed all Russian troops about to fall on Persia, to leave.

It is not that they would lose. He hated conflicts. Paul I was more enemies than he made friendships despite all of his diplomatic, chivalric reforms. It seems that very few people loved him. It was partly because of his behavior. He became so infatuated with his position after he got it.

Although he might have been a tyrant in some ways, it isn't important that he made Russia fall, as one would expect. He is actually a diplomat and has good relations with many countries. Unfortunately, his assassination occurred in 1801. Alexander I of Russia was his only son.

Alexander took on the expansionist mentality of Catherine. Alexander was also a strong advocate for education. He established three more Russian universities. He enjoyed literature and science, two fields that flourished while he was in power.

While Catherine died, the development of Imperial Russia continued long after her death. It culminated with Alexander I, Russia's reign, winning over Napoleon's armies. All things considered Imperial Russia represents the one period in Russian history which was not drowned with blood and internal and exterior conflicts. It marks the moment when Russia gave up on its ambition to become a military power and instead aimed to become an intellectual force. We will be discussing how this will affect the next period.

A time in which the so called "wooden mouth" ruled, and where there was limited freedom of expression, whether it be in domestic life, or in the arts, the period immediately after the Russian Revolution has been the most scrutinized, criticized, and praised. The Russian Empire lasted till 1917 when it became a Republic. Russia was known for its "Russian Soviet Federative Socialist Republic" which existed from 1917 to 1920. The Soviet Union was established in 1922.

Common Misconceptions We Didn't Know Were Right

* "Russia's in Europe, not Asia" is half the truth. Not many people know that Russia can be found in both Europe (and Asia) if asked. Russia is such large that anything west from the Urals is European Russia, and everything on the east Asian Russia.

* Another common misconception was that Imperial Russia's military judge were bloodthirsty or servile. They would often sentence anyone

who was suspected of treason. Truth be told, although Russia's law allowed for military death they would also inquire in the courts and prison was always preferable to execution.

Trivia: Imperial Russia

* The Russian Empire possessed a total area of 228,000,000 km2, which is one the largest in history.

* 69.3%, or 69.3%, of the Empire's inhabitants were Orthodox Christians. Muslims, 11.1%, held the second place.

* Many of Peter's political reforms remain in place within the Russian government at the 21st-century.

If you could choose

* If Peter The Great were alive, would you be so brave to assume the leadership role?

* Would Catherine the Great have been proud of you as a female for having the strength to handle so many conflict situations?

* If Paul I was in power, would you have called off the troops about persisting?

Questionnaire:

1. Who unified all the Russian Appanages?

2. How many years has the Great Northern War lasted?

3. When did Catherine of the Great rise to power?

Chapter 9: The Russian Revolution (and the Creation of the Soviet Union)

In 1917, Russia's Empire collapsed, and Nicholas II of Russia was forced to abdicate. His coronation was prophetic about the outcome of Nicholas II's regency. Nearly 1,400 were trampled on Khodynka Field by the 30th of Mai 1896. The reason they were trampled to death was that they were supposed to receive food as presents. These deaths are not related to Nicholas II. It was apparent from the very beginning that Nicholas did not have any political experience.

Tens of thousands of Russians lost their lives during the Russo-Japanese War. It took place in 1904-1905. Nicholas II was largely responsible, since the Russian army suffered multiple defeats. It was also obvious that sending more troops on to the battlefield was like sending milk to the slaughterhouse.

In 1905 around 1000 people died as a result of the "Bloody Sunday" when the Imperial Guard opened fired on demonstrators. Many other deaths, including those linked to Nicholas II were also caused by "pogroms," which were persecutions of various ethnic groups within a nation. In this example, the Russian empire received the Partitions of Poland territories in 1772.

History tends to overlook the fact Nicholas II was explicitly anti-Semitic. Although these conflicts did NOT escalate to the global level of anti-Semitism in Hitler's Germany, people still lost lives. In 1911, Nicholas the Tsar makes his first steps toward abolition of these programs. They did nothing to achieve his ultimate goal of unifying Russians. He was never forgiven by the Russians. He had indulged in anti-Semitism much too long in order not to be convicted.

What is commonly called the "Russian Revolution" was actually actually a series (2) revolutions. One happened in February and one later in October. Although the causes of the riots were many, it's generally agreed that World War I's terrible consequences was a major trigger.

Nicholas II was a weak military leader. Nicholas II's incompetent leadership led to the death of over 3,3 million Russians during World War 1. It is one thing to send skilled troops to war. They have a real chance to actually come back. Nicholas II didn't do it. He instead sent to war all people who could possess a firearm, even farmers. In this manner, being summoned was a certain death-warrant.

Nicholas II of Russia was unfit to be ruler and he was accused in Russia of leading its people to the edge. His management style of the army was far too inefficient to be effective. This led to the deaths and suffering of millions. The German forces defeated the Russian troops with brutal efficiency. Russian people couldn't bow down to a ruler that showed no understanding of his duties.

The 1stRevolution-23 February 1917

Nicholas II's war tactic of sending everyone to the front meant that very few Russians were able to work the land, and provide food for millions. The prices continued rising, resulting in Russia being plunged into chaos and ruining its economy's foundations. Russia has had many famines during its history. It was now dangerously close for another. It would have been worse if there was a bomb in the political arena that was set to go off much sooner than expected.

Russians found their last straw in Nicholas II's apathetic silence. Soon enough they began rioting in order to pillage food stores. Although they were told to stop the violence (shooting blindly at protesters), the police and army only eventually agreed with them. They had lost all respect for the royal orders, and this is not surprising.

Petrograd, Russia's former capital, was forced to boil for one week. The interesting thing to remember is that the reason for this mutiny could not be determined. It happened completely by accident, though all the negative aspects surrounding Nicholas' reign were undoubtedly a factor. Russian people began to hate Nicholas Tsar and became more bitter. They wanted him out. They couldn't be blamed.

Workers, soldiers, ordinary men and others joined together in an act that was unmatched and led to protests against the war. Russians had hoped that the Russian ProvisionalGovernment would be able to save them from conflict after the death and burial of Emperor Nicholas II. But it was clear that this government waged war every day.

Russia would have collapsed from the inside if this sequence of devastating events continued. This was not an unusual event in Russia's long history. However, this time the situation was different. The Russian people were tired of being led to destruction after disaster. They wanted change. And they wanted it fast.

Russians requested Nicholas I's immediate abdication. Russia would have entered Civil War if Nicholas II had not abdicated. Nicholas II applied for shelter in Britain, but was denied. He and his relatives were arrested and imprisoned. They were then executed on the 17th, July 1918. Russia was still far from settling its differences, though the Tsarist autocracy was also overthrown.

His family, Tsar Nicholas, were made into passion bearers. The title is granted to people who have had a martyrlike death. The reign of the Tsar shows that he is not the martyr that the Church has portrayed him to have been. Even some Church members opposed his sainthood for obvious reason. First of all, a martyr can only be declared if the victim was killed because he or she refused to abandon their religion. His entire family was executed alongside him. Nicholas II was not holy. However, his incompetence as ruler over the Russian Empire reached celestial heights.

The number of contestants who took the harnesses for the Empire and then so many sides was so high that "confusing", while it may be confusing, does not reflect the actual atmosphere that surrounded Russia back then. Some Russians knew the outcome, but most didn't. So they chose the side offering more advantages. When people are dispersed, the leader that pays attention and sees everything is usually the one that is most rewarded at the end of the pandemonium. Vladimir Lenin, undoubtedly one of the most important historical figures in the Russian Revolution, was that person.

1917 was another miserable year. Estonians voted for autonomy. Georgy Lvov became Head of the Provisional Government. Alexander Kerensky soon replaced him. Also, the army deserts from the front under the threat of death. Clashes break up almost everywhere. Undoubtedly, Russia's Provisional Government was as weak as the Emperor. The Russians refused to take it. The Russian Social Democratic Party was far more capable of leading than the Provisional Government. Or at least that is their belief.

The Bolshevik revolution is next.

The 2nd Revolution- 25th Oct 1917

Knowing that the Provisional Government established on Nicholas II's abdication was at the opposite extreme of Soviets is key to understanding why the Bolshevik revolt took place. One of many reasons the Bolshevik revolution caused anger among the population was that they did not have any land and that the Government didn't want to grant it. Vladimir Lenin saw in it the chance to do the things he had been planning while on exile: get all the people behind him and start the revolution.

On October 25th, the Bolsheviks stormed the Government Buildings, including the Winter Palace. This was also the Russian Provisional Government's Headquarters. It was extremely poorly protected, which allowed for a relatively peaceful exchange of power. Most people who were in the Palace left when asked. Bolsheviks had portrayed a moment that was heroic but the reality wasn't so.

As you may already know, Lenin was one of the key figures in this uprising - he was its leader. He had expressed his disapproval for the Tsarist monarchy and encouraged people against it since 1905. However, the revolution planned for that same year was canceled. There were many uprisings. However, people weren't quite as united in their efforts as Lenin desired.

The 1905 revolution was quickly ended by the establishment of both the State Duma in Kazakhstan and the Russian Constitution one year later. The Russian Constitution was a reformulation and adaptation of the 1832-era book of laws. Lenin was unable to plan for a huge overthrow. This abrupt conclusion ended his plans. Lenin did NOT advise the people to remain put or to retreat when Nicholas II and his guards opened fire upon the protesters at Bloody Sunday. He wanted them strike back. It would have prevented a revolution in 1917. And the tsarist government would have been decimated much more quickly. The Secret Police or Okhrana began to hunt down those who had instigated insurrection.

It isn't surprising that Lenin was exiled incitement. He traveled throughout Europe for ten long years, seeking asylum mainly in Finland. His vision of the proletariat rising up and breaking its chains never faded. He wrote for many publications and traveled to London, Munich, Geneva, and London. This helped instill the same pride in the proletariat as the one that would explode in 1917. One of his most famous pamphlets was "What's to be done?" It was published 1902 and was influential for many, including the future tyrant Joseph Stalin.

Because the situation had changed significantly, he returned back to Russia in 1918 and encouraged Russians to take final steps in overthrowing and replacing the Provisional Government by the Communist Party. He was able to quickly get into the Finland Station in Petrograd to train all the Bolsheviks for the insurrection spirit. He took advantage the chaos of the country's involvement with the 1st World War, which was just beginning, and gave speeches to many meetings. His long-awaited crusade was finally realized. He spent most of his time giving speeches to win people and going to Bolshevik Central Committee gatherings.

He had a secret weapon: he was able to return to Russia at the right time when Russians were ready to endorse his almost prophetic enterprise. But that was not all. He had to flee back to Finland for a few more times, as he was being followed by the Police. He never stopped fighting, even though he was far away. He continued writing manifestos. Mensheviks were beginning to clash with Bolsheviks more or less outlandishly. Lenin grabbed the opportunity, went back to Russia, and called for a meeting at the Bolshevik Committee. A majority of the people supported the decision to get guns and march towards Winter Palace.

One could not have anticipated the five years of violence and internal discord that would follow. Lenin never imagined that he would instigate an insurrection against headquarters of the Provisional Government.

The Aftermath

After the Provisional Government collapsed, the Soviet Government, led Vladimir Lenin, took over. Despite a fervent resistance from the Bolsheviks, they were defeated by the people. The uncertainty of the Russian future caused the Russian Civil War (1917-1922). On the one side, there were Russians that didn't have anything to do with the Soviet Government. Others believed that there would have been better command by other factions.

In a nutshell, there were Communists and passionate Anti-Communists. The Red Army was led by Vladimir Lenin as Bolsheviks. The White Army was represented by other factions. This conflict will help pave the way to the Soviet Union.

The Civil war was a disaster in the history of the White Army. The Red Army was better organised and many people sided. Bolsheviks got Russia rid from the inefficient Provisional Govt, so they were automatically considered to be the good guys. Others sided against them as fast as they could. The White Army, which included capitalists, monarchists and socialists (albeit of a different sort than Lenin), won the victory. He had likely not anticipated such a wide opposition. The Red Scare was launched quickly. Lenin hoped to rid the world of any uprisings by means of the Red Scare.

A total of 7 million White Army soldiers died at the hands communists, giving you a glimpse of the larger picture. This was a mere 1 million soldiers compared to the horrendous losses suffered by the anti communist armies. Other than the battle of the Red armies, many independent groups fought against Russia for their independence.

One such group was the Green Army. This, in turn, was primarily made up of peasants that didn't trust governments who were trying to dominate. They often fought one another and both Red and White army. It was a maelstrom of fighting that made it difficult for anyone to know who they were fighting. The Civil War merited attention from other leaders as well. If the Red Army were to win, it would only have meant that Communism could have reached other nations sooner or later. This was something which had to be stopped before too much was done. This is where the Red Scare originated, it is not hard to believe.

Japan, Canada France France, Italy, Canada, France, USA and UK joined the Civil War in support of the White Army. The Red Scare had no place in Europe, and it had to end. This time is known as "The Siberian Intervention", which lasted for a period of 1918-1922. When the Civil

War ended, it was called the Siberian Intervention. All the countries mentioned participated in the War. Japan, which sent approximately 70,000 soldiers, provided the greatest aid. The United States sent about 8000 troops, while the rest sent just 2,500. France was at the bottom of the list with just 800 soldiers.

With all the destruction, the Civil War had terrible consequences. There was famine. There were millions homeless children on the streets in Russia. Factories were demolished. Inadequate sanitation systems led to epidemics of disease. Typhus killed 3 million people in the United States 2 years before World War II. Producing goods was almost impossible since all crops were destroyed.

Despite the fact that many nations fought alongside the White Army and won, the Red Army won. This led to another terrible period in Russia's already ruinous past: the Soviet Union. These terrible outcomes of Civil War were made very painfully apparent during this period.

It appears that each stage of Russian historical history inherits the worst traits and characteristics of its predecessor. Every stage is marked by bloodshed, which leaves traces in the history books. Change in other European nations was often at a lower price, but in Russia it was always the most expensive. It proves Russia's uniqueness in European history in this regard.

The Soviet Union -- 1922

The Soviet Union had 15 Soviet republics. It also included 15 independent states. It functioned as an empire-like mega-country. The 28th Dec 1922 is when the Union was founded. It will exist until 1991. Vladimir Lenin served as the Soviet Union's head for two years from 1922 until 1924, when his death occurred. Joseph Stalin will be his successor.

Stalin was born in 1878. Karl Marx's Capital, and socialism generally, have been influencing him ever since he grew up. His career in politics started soon after. He frequently incited people to take action through socialism that had such an effect on his personal life. He became the USSR's premier from 1941-1953.

Stalin was also an important part of the revolutions in 1917, but his name will not be known until 1924. His Soviet Union leadership remained in history as one among the most totalitarian regimes ever placed on people. Some people view him as a good person, but the opinions of the west world and the rest Europe are very different. He is generally considered a tyrant who caused more casualties than Hitler. His extreme views and unconventional methods caused famine in the 1930s and forced many to work.

After being made leader of Communist Party, the Collectivization was initiated. The Collectivization made all that was cultivated or grown on farms the property and the property the state. Russians received low wages. Their motivation to work was slowed by the fact that their crops became the state's. The Collectivization turned out to be less efficient than Stalin had predicted.

Many people stole food during this time. This is understandable since they were provided with food that was not sufficient for just one person. A serious offense against the system was keeping food from your own crops and meat from other animals. The food you ate was not yours. Everything that was grown belonged to the government. Every person, farmer or not, had to work for Stalin. Needless to mention, this made work less satisfying than it used to when workers could eat the food they earned.

This process of collectivization didn't have a limited impact on Russia. It also took effect in Yugoslavia. Hungary. Bulgaria. This forced labor was applied to every state that was affected by the Soviet Union. Contrariwise with what Stalin had hoped for when he created the Five-Year Plan this did not result to large-scale agricultural production. It caused a poor economy and human suffering instead.

The Collectivization took effect simultaneously with Stalin's attempt to force industrialization. As a result, millions died of starvation. Gulags took the lives of millions of others who were forced into work. According to several sources, Stalin is believed to have killed more people than other dictators. His rule lasted 30 years, making it easy to believe the claim. He is also known for having killed anyone who tried to oppose his rule. This is a trait that many rulers before he had. Nicholas II, for one, used to shut down the mouths his political adversaries by having them executed.

Towards World War II

World War II began in 1939. It quickly escalated into one of the most bloody conflicts in history. Russia was a communist republic, and the Nazis were hostile to this ideology. Germany was also paranoid, believing that the Soviet Union was soon to join the opposition. As a result, relations between these two nations began to decline. Perhaps the word "decayed" is a misnomer. Germany always saw Soviet Union as a great capture. Despite the fact that a neutrality accord was quickly signed between Germany and the USSR, the former suffered immense losses. To some degree, this pact wasn't really a pretext but was meant to give Hitler enough time for his almost apocalyptic plan.

While it appeared that everything was going as planned, with Hitler and Stalin seemingly communicating diplomatically to one another, the truth was that the secret situation was completely different behind the curtains. The World War II had the potential to forever change Russia's face. An amazing fact to mention is that Russia probably survived World War II because it was used in living in difficult times. It had seen more hardships than many European countries. It had survived bloodshed, famines, and mutiny that it became trivial. However, having survived them all would be crucial in its survival, as you will see.

Russians understood how to survive without much, which enabled them to take on the Germans fully. Despite Russia suffering from the Collectivization its economy was far from perfect but it proved to be a key factor in the defeat by the Nazi forces. The USSR, while a dyadic historical subject, is still a significant one in that it was hated far more than any other. It would not have been possible for Europe to exist today without them.

You might have come across misinformation

* Some people believe that the Communist regime required people to wait in long lines to buy toilet papers. This is false. Yes, there were lines just like today's in America to get to different shops and places. But it wasn't for toilet paper, or any other basic necessity.

* Another misconception about Russia is that it is still a communist land. This is incorrect. Russia is a democratic democracy, and has been since 1991 when Boris Yeltsin won the election to be its president. While Russia isn't as powerful as other

democratic countries in democracy, it is a state that is able to hold its own. But, one thing is sure: it is no longer a communist nation. Today there is more freedom than ever before. Press freedom is the most restricted thing.

* A second misconception claims that the Russian Revolution took places on November 7. While it is possible to be incorrect, it is not true. It all depends what calendar you choose. It is recorded on the Julian calendar as the 25th Oct., while it is noted on the Gregorian schedule as the 7th Nov.

Facts About the Soviet Union

* 80% of a whole generation of men from the Soviet Union were killed in WWII.

* The Soviet Constitution, which contained 72 articles, was drafted in 1924.

* A thing known as Neo-Stalinism.

If You Could Choose

* Lenin's plan to make the proletariat more prosperous was abandoned in 1905. If you were him, would your plans have been abandoned or would you have kept working?

* What would your actions have been if you had the title of Tsar Nicholas 2? Would you have sent experienced people to the front believing you could win, or would it have called for a general retreat?

* Would the Christianization and renaming of the late Tsar have made you a better choice?

Questionnaire:

1. When did the first revolution occur?

2. Who was Bolsheviks' leader?

3. Why was Nicholas II of Russia forced by force to abdicate

4. What does Collectivization actually stand for?

Chapter 10: World War II

World War II started in September 1939. It ended six year later, September 2, 1945. It was the most bloody armed conflict that has ever occurred in human history. Tens of millions of people died worldwide. The "Holocaust," Hiroshima," and "Nagasaki" incidents still have the power to make our skin crawl. World War II was the first instance of nuclear weapons being used in history. The war began when Germany invaded Poland. It was ruled by Adolf Hitler, who had visions of immortal glory and was unhinged.

The entire world was involved in the conflict. However, without the sacrifices made during World War II by the Soviet Union, the world would be very different today. This is not an exaggeration. This is the undisputed truth and we will offer many reasons why.

WWII was fought against two major forces. They had more or less the same objectives.

* The Allies, The United States of America. Great Britain. Soviet Union. China.

* The Axis, Germany, Italy, Japan. The Soviet Union was considered the Axis' arch enemy.

Hitler and Stalin shared a close friendship at the beginning of the war. Hitler's astonishingly rapid rise in power and the imminent threat that he would be destroyed by the Nazis, made it imperative for the Soviet Union to sign the Molotov-Ribbentrop Pact, which was signed on the 23rd August 1939. The non-aggression Pact was then respected for two more years.

One of the errors made by the Soviet Union was to keep the pact secret. The Allies were not pleased when the USSR revealed this "trivial aspect" to them. This will be one of the main justifications for Cold War, which began right after World War II ended.

The USSR could have predicted that the pact wouldn't be kept. There are traces of Hitler's desire conquer the world as far back at 1925 when he wrote Mein Kampf (his controversial autobiography). Slavics, as well as Jews and most Eastern European peoples were considered Untermenschen by Hitler. Although it did provide safety for the USSR, Ribbentrop and Molotov were a disaster.

Hitler broke off the pact, activated Operation Barbarossa to invade the Soviet Union. The invasion unleashed 4 million Axis Soldiers. The Soviet Union was literally hanging on a thread after some victories by the Germans. Hitler underestimated Stalin despite the fact that he was willing and able to do so much to favor the Axis. His Order No. His Order No. To be honest, 227 was radical. The Red Army declared the latter a death threat and made it mandatory that all soldiers surrender. The Red Army faced a death penalty with the threat of being killed if it attempted to retreat in the face from the Germans, further strengthening the motivation.

It is said that the German invasion was the largest in history. However, if we were to consider the largest mobilization, it would have to be the USSR. An encouragement program that encouraged people to "fight till the death, until the last" was so important that it obscured the importance and importance of military strategy. It worked.

Stalin did not react correctly at first. This resulted in 4 million Soviet Union soldiers being killed and around 3 million being taken prisoner in order to await their fate in the German concentration camp. It was not the end. The Soviet Union was able to escape from the Nazi threat, and gave the Allies the opportunity to destroy them.

How the Soviet Union Overcame Hitler and the Nazis

The Soviet Union and its ideology on warfare are the keys to understanding how it helped the world eradicate the Nazi menace. As we have seen, Russia has become a huge power by acquiring and integrating new territories. This is exactly how it could defeat the Nazi army and not fall under its weight. It actually turned the tides of war around 360 degrees.

The Russian army was never designed to be used for defensive purposes. The result is that an army designed for defense is weaker than one designed to prove the country is unprepared for serious conflict.

Stalin, like the other leaders before, taught it to be an offensive force to be reckoned, a warmachine to support the expansionist ideology. Hitler seemed to forget this fact when Operation Barbarossa was launched. He didn't anticipate that the Soviet Union would mobilize its large army and move the German forces towards Berlin.

History is often objective. Stalin may have been an aristocrat, but his ability to demolish Hitler's plans should be praised. Hitler underestimated again the Union's power and the Soviet Union was mobilized in 1941. Hitler ordered Moscow's attack as the Wehrmacht was closing down on Moscow.

1) The Soviet army was outnumbered by its reserves and had no reserves

2) his own forces were able see it through, though the Nazis had suffered great losses due to their inability to prepare for the Russian winter.

His calculations proved to be disastrous. Stalin built an army almost as large and powerful as Hitler in just a short period. Hitler was too consumed with his Westward expansion to care about the German issue. Stalin more than doubled the size of his army over this time. The Soviet Union launched an invasion attack against Germany to retake the German forces.

Two of Europe's largest forces collided, sending tidal winds through Europe. During WWII it was just the USSR versus Germany. The fight was so fierce that no one could know with certainty which of them would win. You could think of this as a game in chess. It is often reminiscent wars and strategies used during wars. The USSR waited until Germany had consumed all of its pieces and then set in motion its final strategy.

Retaliation from the Soviet Union

Hitler's Operation Typhoon aimed to occupy Moscow. He was met with more resistance then he had anticipated. This operation, meant to turn Moscow to dust and toashes, saw approximately 2,000,000 German soldiers involved. They were supported by a thousand Panzer-tanks. These tanks did not assist in conquering the city. It seemed that they were within arm's distance. The Soviet forces were not nearly as exhausted than the German. Stalin summoned troops from other regions, especially the Far Eastern or Siberian. Hitler was unaware of these armies.

Also, the weather played a key role. The ground was muddy from the snow, which slowed German forces. The Germans were being harassed more than they were actually fighting. Stalin still had time to transform all the factories into weapon-making facilities.

Moscow was actually preparing its troops, even though certain divisions had been fighting in Bryansk/Vyazma. Hitler thought he was going down on Moscow. But Hitler failed to take into account something very important. He claimed Moscow was giving up its last breath to give the Russians the motivation they needed to save their heritage from certain Nazi destruction. The Red Army grew in strength and was supported by the other districts mentioned.

Heinz WilhemGuderian became the general responsible for the attack on Moscow. After months of difficulties, the Germans were unable to advance due to the weather and the constant stream of Soviet reinforcements. The Soviet Union started its offensive right around the time. Nearly 1 million Red Army soldiers were mobilized against the static Wehrmacht. This forced it to withdraw.

Hitler ordered the Wehrmacht against all odds to defend its positions and stopped the inefficient defense. Despite this, Red Army managed 250 km to push the Germans from Moscow. Needless, the Western world was stunned as it seemed impossible for the Soviet Union to escape Hitler's wrath.

It is one moment in history that stands out, and it's very close to what many people, whether they are religious or secular, consider a "miracle." Hitler did not consider many factors when he broke Ribbentrop–Molotov's pact. By thinking that the German army was "invincible" and the Red Army is weak and fearful, Hitler jeopardized his own safety.

The USSR was unable to defeat the Germans despite its best efforts. Hitler was fond of "scorched ground," which is the act of burning everything to their ground, from fountains to homes, shelters, and crops during an army's retreat so that they don't have the resources to pursue them further. This was his same tactic used in Northern Finland where the Red Army had to breathe on the necks of the German army. The Nazi tanks destroyed almost half of the buildings.

USSR was reduced down to a mass of steaming concrete, fire, water, and blood. It would take decades before it would rebuild itself. Russia was the only country to be completely destroyed by World War II. This is why the USSR is a hero, at least within the context of this short-lived end of the world. Fortunately, the USSR began a new journey after the war that provided a better life for its citizens.

The Soviet Union after WWII

The Soviet Union suffered most of the World War II casualties. The Allies did not stop Hitler's plans. However, the USSR was devastated. More than half of the country was in ruin after the war, which saw 40 million people lose their lives. As one might expect, the economy was in tethers. Stalin had transformed everything in a gun making factory. In light of the sheer volume of German forces, this was a wise decision.

Furthermore, millions upon millions of soldiers during WWII had to be fed, properly equipped, and taken care when they got hurt. Russians too needed food to support their families.

1948: The Marshall Plan gave financial aid to rebuilding nations in the aftermath of World War II. However, the Soviet Union refused the opportunity to be part of the program. As we'll see, this move created tensions between both superpowers in the future.

The USSR did NOT see this "help" as a legitimate interest in funding the reconstruction of the country. Therefore, The Marshall Plan was more like a plot to weaken the USSR, and the USSR's control over all other countries. The Marshall Plan was rejected by the USSR, so the USSR devised its own plan. This was called "The Molotov Plan". This was a paradoxical and controversial course of action. First of all, the USSR had fallen into ruin and asked for economic assistance from the Axis countries. Second, it helped Eastern Bloc nations, though it was far removed from being in a position that it could offer it without experiencing an economic collapse.

Great Britain and Sweden offered assistance. Another source of help was the Union's occupied countries from WWII. Many German soldiers were ordered to do forced labor by the Yalta

Conference. 4 million Soviet Union prisoners labored to rebuild the Soviet Union.

Stalin died in 1953. The Soviet Union went through a series political reforms. Germany underwent a similar process, called "denazification". This was after the "unconditional surrender," stipulated at the Yalta Conference. Nikita Shrushchev became leader of the Union and remained there until 1964. He was the one who began the. He was an inefficient leader. Many reforms he implemented had little or no effect on the Soviet Union.

Khrushchev and the de-StalinizationProcess

Many of his enemies were made by the de-Stalinization process. He was appointed to the position of leadership after the tales from the Gulags became a common theme, and many of his political POWs had been released. Khrushchev did see Stalin not as an hero but as criminal. He spent most of his leadership debunking Stalin's war crimes. It is possible that he did it to rally his people, but he was unwilling to denounce the Soviet Union. This furthered the Cold War's symptoms.

Khrushchev was seen in this way as a leader who attempted to force the USSR towards Western Ideals. Khrushchev had opened the doors to tourists, which supported the idea. The USSR was then flooded with them. The Russian people were shocked to find so much diversity but also deceit.

Khrushchev also launched a massive agricultural campaign. He apparently wanted corn in USSR. Iowa, the biggest corn-producing state in America, was home to the United States. Khrushchev desired the USSR to reach the same heights. However, the USSR didn't have favorable weather conditions that could have facilitated this agricultural growth. This led to a loss of a lot money due to utopic views and inefficient spending.

Khrushchev was also trying to compete with America, this time in the dairy product production. This was disastrous - food prices rose dramatically and there was even rebellion against the authorities. Approximately 150 people were either killed, imprisoned, or executed. Khrushchev was once a "lackey", and this proved to be a mistake. Khrushchev suffered from hunger shortly afterward. His approval rating was even worse because he spent too much money to try and improve the USSR's agriculture output. When he could have just purchased the products.

Nikita Chrushchev also tried reforms in education. However, he was unsuccessful at their implementation. He advocated for a transfer of higher education from cities to the rural centers. The academic intelligence opposed this vehemently. Khrushchev became more West-oriented than the USSR. Khrushchev started the "vocational schools" that were meant to revive skills and inspire youth to learn. This worked in the short term. School attendance increased. In the end, though, the rural education which he hoped to improve failed and many of the children who came from villages never went to school.

An organized group of conspirators forced Khrushchev from office. He had lost the support both of his Russian friends and of his closest family members. He felt that all of this was a good thing and took pride in exposing Joseph Stalin's bloodthirsty nature.

To the dissolution the Union, there were four other leaders. From 1964 until 1982, Leonid Brezhnev served. Leonid didn't try to make all the important decisions like Khrushchev. This didn't work out for him. Because he wanted to improve the USSR's growth, he began the Era of Stagnation. This was a disaster for society as a whole and politics. Brezhnev supported Khrushchev during his time in office and strongly opposed his denigrations of Stalin's methods. After Khrushchev's resignation, things changed dramatically when Brezhnev became a very conservative leader.

Yuri Andropov, who succeeded Brezhnev, came to power in 1982. He served up until 1984, and was then replaced by Konstantin Chernenko. Mikhail Gorbachev was his last successor, and he served in office from 1991 to 1990.

After the war, Soviet Union slowly rebuilt itself and began to integrate the countries it conquered as a way of stopping Hitler's expansion. Romania, Poland Hungary Czechoslovakia Czech Republic Albania, Romania and other countries were all under Soviet control until 1991.

The Soviet Union entered a period called the "Cold War" in 1947. It is believed that Russia is still trapped in this period because of ongoing tensions and hostilities with the United States of

America. The Cold War did nothing to imply an open, armed conflict. However, it did imply a quiet distrust and scrutiny between the two superpowers. You can clearly see that claims that Cold War is in its brunt still today are not exaggerated.

These Misconceptions Could Have Been Heard

Russian people view Mikhail Gorbachev to be a hero. Russians claim that this is a lie. Although people outside Russia may be fascinated by him but Russians regard him as the one who has brought ruin to their economy.

* Another misconception is that Russia has lost its economy and it won't recover soon. While this may seem true, it was proven that the Russian people were able to get the ball rolling in innovation and boosting their economy. They were able to climb to the top thanks to their vast human resources.

Russia's efforts helped win World War II in Europe. Although Russia won, it wasn't the only country that was victorious. Many countries made great sacrifices to win this war.

Facts About the Soviet Union in WWII

* Most historians agree the German invasion wasn't surprising. Stalin, however, was unwilling to believe Hitler would end the pact.

* The majority of people believed that the Nazis would erase Soviet Union from the world map.

* Weather, apart from quick thinking and war tactics was the main factor in Germany's defeat of the Soviet Union.

What would You Do?

* Stalin failed, or did not want Hitler to see his intentions. Is it possible that you would have prepared yourself for the invasion, even if you weren't there?

* Would Stalin's instructions to soldiers not surrender have been followed or would you have had the courage to flee from the army as a soldier?

* What would Khrushchev do differently if given the chance?

Questionnaire:

1. What was it called the neutrality deal between Germany, the Soviet Union and other countries?

2. What countries were part Axis member countries?

3. Which countries were Allies member?

4. What kinda ideology did Joseph Stalin have in the Soviet Union?

Chapter 11: Cold War

The Cold War began right after the 2nd World War ended. The Cold War was not referred to as "War", but it did not escalate into an actual armed conflict. It was shared by both America and Soviet Union.

Although the two countries had fought sidebyside in WWII, the relationship between them was far less cordial than it was even then. Their trust in each other was further diminished by a variety.

* The delayed Normandy Landings (the infamous D-Day), Stalin believed was a plot by the Nazis to see the Soviet Union be crushed under their feet.

* The United States was not a fan of Joseph Stalin's methods. He was viewed as a dictator, and the ideology he promoted was deplorable.

* As early as 1917, the USA became increasingly paranoid, and started propagandizing against communism.

* Great Britain was not keen to forget that, on the onset WWII, the Soviet Union had made a neutrality deal with Hitler.

In reality, the Cold War was not about Soviet Union versus United States but about Communism or Capitalism. Two opposing ideologies. These inequalities existed even though they were not as clear during the 2nd World War. For the Alliance's success, the states had the responsibility to disarm the hatchet or act as if they didn't exist.

"Espionage", and "nuclear weaponry" are redundant in the contexts of the Cold War. Each side blamed another for developing nuclear weapons and engaging in spying. Red Scare is another term used to discuss the Cold War.

The Iron Curtain

1945 was the year that the Soviet Union established the Iron Curtain. This boundary was to protect the Union against the west, as well the other states not in its possession. Iron Curtain was both a metaphorical representation and a physical one. The Iron Curtain was an iron barrier that separated Western Europe and Soviet Union.

The 1989 uprising against Communism led to the destruction of the Soviet Union. The Iron Curtain was not able to alleviate the anxiety and tension in the relationship between the US Soviet Union. However, it did enhance them.

The Red Scare

The United States ran a vast anti-Soviet propaganda campaign called the Red Scare. The Red Scare began as a deliberate and paranoid reaction towards Communism. It was exacerbated in part by false claims or legends. Rumors claimed that the US was full of Soviet spies. The Soviet Union however warned against American spying.

The Soviet Union did not possess nuclear weapons until 1949. However, things changed quickly to the shock and terror of the American people. 1949 was an extremely difficult year for America. The Russians had tested their first nuke weapon. In the Chinese Civil War, the Communist Party of China was the victor. There had been so much hysteria at American soil since the Salem Witch Trials. And it clearly affected relations between the US Soviet Union.

The Cold War of 1953 and 1957

The Soviet Union had its own ideology in the countries that it occupied and won following

WWII, further complicating the Cold War. This was considered a grave problem by the Americans and British. All Eastern Europe would be under the Soviet Union's rule. This could not have happened.

However, the fear subsided when Joseph Stalin died in 1953. Nevertheless, the Red Scare had done more to America than to Soviet Union. The latter was not paranoid or distrustful for some reason. While the Cold War may have been over now that Stalin had died, it was not over. Then came an event that demonstrated that the USSR and Soviet Union were miles away from reaching an agreement. This is commonly referred to as a proxy conflict in which both parties tried to prove one another that they were not to budge.

The Vietnam War

Contrary to WWII and WWII, the Vietnam War saw US and Soviet Union at opposite ends of the front. While the Soviet Union was able to support North Vietnam, the United States was able to support South Vietnam. The war started in November 1955, and ended twenty years later, on April 30, 1975.

We said that the Vietnam war was a proxy conflict. This allowed for the Soviet Union to act as an ally in North Vietnam and fight against the US. Because it was siding in South Vietnam, the US was also doing the same.

This could have been a pretext for open-armed warfare between these two powers since the Cold War. It was a way for them to get some much-needed steam. The US could have used the nuclear bomb even if the Soviet Union wouldn't have intervened in Vietnam War. The possibility of triggering World War III by doing this while the Communists from the Union were present is possible. The United States thought about using nuclear attacks, but they voted to stop them.

Gorbachev's Role in Ending Cold War

Mikhail Gorbachev became the Soviet Union's final leader and was responsible for putting the final nail in the coffin. He was made the leader of the Soviet Union in 1990, just one years before it collapsed. He quickly proposed a number of reforms to facilitate the normalization of relations with America, which led to the close of the Cold War.

He introduced Perestroika as well as the Soviet Union to Glasnost. These were two of his most important initiatives. Prior to Glasnost, Russians didn't have freedom of speech and were not open for Western influence. Gorbachev made that change in 1988. The freedom to have your own business was something that has been denied for many years.

Perestroika was the closest that the Soviet Union came to democracy. Perestroika was both an economic and political revolution. In the end, it was a form Socialism tailored so that the Russians could reap the benefits. Gorbachev hoped to improve relations with Western countries through diplomacy. He proposed that Russia should be stripped of certain parts of its nuclear arsenal, but only if the US agreed to do the same.

It is clear to see why Cold War was nearing its end. America was indeed a fan of Gorbachev's reforms. The Soviet leader was able to accomplish reasonable things, but the Russians failed to see his moves clearly. Gorbachev rescinded the Brezhnev doctrine on 1988. This only caused a series Russian mutinies.

The Eastern Bloc collapsed quickly because not many other countries were as open for change as Gorbachev. The Soviet Union gave people a bitter taste of the relative democracy. It made them feel like they were losing the life they loved. The Soviet Union had been heavily involved in Afghanistan and so the economy was still a problem. The Soviet Union continued to fall apart, threatening its dissolution.

1989 saw the Soviet Union be effected by a series revolutions, which suggested the end of Communism. It started in Poland. Later, it was extended to Bulgaria, Romania Czechoslovakia, East Germany and Hungary.

The End Of the Cold War

Gorbachev's reforms gave rise to the suspicion that the Cold War would be ending. It is obvious why: The Soviet Union, under Gorbachev, was not seen to be an imminent threat for the United States. The fear about a Communist invasion subsided greatly. Gorbachev was not the Soviet despot we are used to believe that the Union has taken the first steps in falling in line.

It was difficult for Americans to get rid of the Cold War mentality they were taught. They had spent years learning how to build bunkers behind their houses. It was many years before the Red Scare really ended the Cold War.

Myths and misconceptions about Russia's Cold War

* The Warsaw Pact was a Treaty of Friendship that included all the countries of the Soviet Union. Many satellite states were also included in the pact but they were not Russian.

* Russia is shorthand for the Soviet Union. But historians would disagree. Russia and Soviet Union have never been the same. The Soviet Union was, for example, formed in 1922 with four republics. Russia made up the largest part. Russia was not part of the Soviet Union.

* Russia, Russian people and American people hate America - or so people believed after the Cold War. The truth is that most Russians are very friendly to American tourists and are curious about American culture. Although they may not feel hatred towards Americans, they aren't anti-American.

Fun facts about the Cold War

* If your Soviet passport hadn't been corroded, it would have been returned to you. Original ones always get corroded.

* Nikita Kharushchev claimed once that Berlin represents the West's testicles. Berlin is the place I go to when I want to make West scream." He was speaking to Mao Zedong, the Chinese revolutionary.

Russia was considered a threat because it sent the first cosmonaut (Yuri Gagarin) into space. The US expected the USSR launch a cosmos-based nuclear warhead.

*

What would YOU do?

* Would it have been possible to accept the Marshall Plan, and avoid the Cold War.

* Would you like to have built the Iron Curtain

Questionnaire:

1. What factors contributed to the establishment and maintenance of the Cold War?

2. Define Red Scare.

3. What were the signs that a Cold War would end, you ask?

4. When did the Cold War come to an end?

Chapter 12: Russia Today's Breakup of the Union

The Soviet Union collapsed after 1989's revolutions. All states that had been part of it were made independent republics. The revolutions ended peacefully for most of them. Romania is the country where revolution ended in the televised executions of Nicolae Ceausescu (and his wife).

On the 8th of Dezember 1991, the Belavezha Accords were signed, making the end of Soviet Union an official matter. The Union was in fact the Russian Federation. Russia, like the other states that were under its control, plunged into financial and political chaos. It was on the verge of economic collapse once more. Boris Yeltsin's leadership caused poverty, crime and high unemployment rates to continue rising.

Post-Soviet Russia under Yeltsin (1991 - 1999)

Boris Yeltsin won the presidency of the Russian Federation after Gorbachev resigned in 1991. A long period of depression followed by his unorthodox reforms of Russia's economy, which led to the collapse of the Federation. Inflation occurred as industries collapsed one after the next. The Russian Federation went from a market economy to an economic one through privatization. But it also ended up in utter economic disaster.

Yeltsin made some good attempts but apparently forgot to recognize that it is not possible to simply create an economic shift without having repercussions. At the end, his popularity was almost zero, but he ran in the second term despite his declining health. He won the second and was named his prime minister. It is likely that he is one of the most famous figures in Russian history: Vladimir Putin.

Yeltsin's presidency wasn't easy. Three enormous issues faced Yeltsin from the very beginning. He had to create a market, offer independence to an empire he had served for so long and finally, establish democracy. After hundreds upon years of oppression, Russians were used to these difficult tasks.

He could have made the Russian people more comfortable, but they had first to understand them. They had been living under an iron fist for so many years. Boris Yeltsin did win his second term. However, a new wave in politico-economic crises occurred, with the most prominent being the Russian Financial Crisis (1998), which saw the government cease to pay its debts through default.

Boris Yeltsin had no choice but to resign following his ineffective second terms and his steadily decreasing popularity. He gave the reins of the leadership to his Prime Minister Vladimir Putin on the 31st and December 1999. Vladimir Putin became president after the 2000 presidential elections.

Present Day of the Russian Federation (from 2000 onwards)

Vladimir Putin was acting president between 1999-2000. He will succeed him as president in 2000. During his two terms in office (2000-2004 & 2004-2008), economic growth was seen in the Russian Federation. Needless to mention, this fact increased the public's trust and demonstrated that Putin was the right man for the job. The living standards rose steadily.

Relations with the West did improve, but only after September 11, 2001, when Putin offered his aid immediately to the US by assisting them in the GWOT. This ongoing conflict continues today. All this led to the resurfacing of decades of bitterness between these states, both having huge nuclear arsenals with different geopolitical aims. The Cold War has a very similar story even today.

One of his first actions during his term as president was to strike an agreement between the oligarchs, which had been created by Yeltsin's privateization. This agreement de-stressed Russia's politics and improved the Federation's sense of financial/economic equity. Putin's second presidential term saw the most significant changes. Putin activated National Priority Projects. This had a positive influence on agriculture and education as well as housing. These initiatives led to increased life expectancy in these areas and improved wages, which was unprecedented since Yeltsin took over.

Vladimir Putin remains one of the most revered and loved Russian leaders. He was Prime Minister for eight years, from 2008 to 2012. This was his third consecutive term as president. He was elected President again in the 2012 elections, and he is still in office. Despite his ability to lead the Russian Federation back from the brink, he has been accused by some of restricting the freedom and expression of the media. Rumours suggest that Vladimir Putin isn't keen on journalists who disagree, regardless of the subject of the discussion.

He was also criticised by the West for annexed Crimea in march 2014. His intervention in Syria's Civil War, which lasted from 2015 to the present, was also disapproved. On closer inspection, the Syrian Civil War functions as another proxy war between the Russian Federation, the United States and is part of what some call the 3rd Cold War.

Despite the protests ongoing in Moscow, Putin's approval ratings are at 86.1% in 2017. The date for next Russia's presidential elections is unknown. Putin may run for his 2nd term. A Russian Federation president is elected to office for six years. This doesn't necessarily apply in other parts of the world.

Russia Misconceptions

* Russia is a country that is irreversible drunkards is the greatest misconception that almost everyone has heard. Rarely are there movies in which a Russian isn't seen carrying a glass of vodka around or being so drunk that his feet can barely support him. This is undoubtedly the most commonly believed lie

about Russia. Scotland and Ireland can prove their dominance anytime.

* Russia has an eternal winter, which would be enough to justify all the alcoholics. This could not be more false. Russia can experience many climates. They would not have made shorts and tshirts if they did. This misperception is meant to be a way for them to display their "political chillness," so it would not be true.

* Putin is highly regarded by Russians. Putin is extremely popular. A lot of people love his charisma and energy. Yet, most Russians don't have the right ideas or are skeptical. Since the Soviets/Tsars ruled them they have realized that making their leanings known is the best way to live a good and happy life.

Modern Russia facts

* Russia is greater than Pluto. Yes, Pluto is larger than Russia. Russia has 17.098.322km2, and Pluto only 16.647.940km2.

* Boris Yeltsin walked once upon a time on Pennsylvania Avenue, Washington D.C. In his underwear. Drunk. He was struggling to get taxis so he could eat pizza.

* Russia has the most nukes in the world, and it would need a protocol to allow it to launch them all.

If the Choice Was Yours

* If Vladimir Putin were you, would your press freedom be greater?

* Would you support the Syrian government, or not?

* If given the chance, would your agreement to join the Global War on terrorism?

Questionnaire:

1. What year was the Belavezha Accords established?

2. When did Boris Yeltsin became president of Russian Federation

3. When did Vladimir Putin become Acting president?

4. When was Russia able to intervene in the Syrian Civil War

What was Russia's Revolution?

The Throne for the Tsar

1917 was the year that the Russian peasants and working class revolted against the injustices and tyranny perpetrated by the ruling classes. They hated especially the Tsar Nicholas II II who was their country's ruler.

There had been a failed revolution attempt in 1905. Tsar Nicholas did create a Duma as a council to the people. This did little to stop the Tsar's ability to control Russia without much influence from his subjects.

Russia was ruled by the Tsar (King). The Tsar was at the top of the military and owned the majority of the land. Even the Church was under the control and supervision of The Tsar.

Nicholas led miserable lives for both the working class, and for peasants. They had no money, lived in desperate conditions and often went hungry.

The ruling class could live in luxury, but the peasants could only be described as slaves. It was true what they said.

Bloody Sunday

In 1905, during the first Revolution, an incident occurred which drew the attention of most working-class Russians toward the Tsar.

A large number marched up to the Tsar's Palace and presented a petition asking for better work conditions. The Tsar did not listen to this peaceful protest. He ordered his soldiers firing on the crowd, killing and wounding many. This is Bloody Sunday.

This is believed to have been a turning-point. The majority of Russians admired the Tsar long before Bloody Sunday. They blamed him for their problems. The marchers wanted him to offer them assistance. After the mass massacre, it was the Tsar who became their enemy. His actions only fuelled growing calls for revolution.

Tsar Nicholas II

Nicholas II was named the last Russian Tsar. He was born in St Petersburg May 18, 1868.

His tutors in private education were very good, but his knowledge about Russian Politics was not that great.

Nicholas married Alexandra from the German royal family. They had five children.

The Russian Royal Families

Nicholas joined Russian Army and rose up to the rank as Colonel. He had a passion to military life but not for politics. This was to prove fatal.

His father was only 26 years old when he died. Nicholas became Nicholas II.

Later, he admitted to a friend he never wanted the title of Tsar since he was not interested "affairs with state".

His rule did not succeed and his attempts at expanding his military reach were stopped when his army surrendered to the Japanese.

Russia's peasant-class was in horrible conditions which led to the rioting.

Although his popularity fell after Bloody Sunday was over, he tried to boost his position by establishing The Duma. It should have been called the Parliament Of the People.

The revolution saw him and his family arrested and held as prisoner of war in 1918.

Russian Revolution 1905

Russia's conditions were extremely harsh at the start of the 1900s. Russia was extremely poor when compared with most of Europe. However the ruling classes (including the Tsar's family) were all extremely wealthy.

France and Britain saw Russia as a backward and undeveloped country. Russia was one last country that maintained serfdom. The system meant that the peasants would be no more than landless slaves forced to work for their masters. This system had vanished from Europe by end of Middle Ages.

Russia abolished the serfdom system on 1861. As it industrialized, it also began to eliminate its serfs. It was the cause of the Revolution in 1905 that gave the serfs freedom. They were able to move freely and organise themselves more freely.

Russia becoming more industrialized, many people fled to cities to work at factories. The new Russian Industrial Workers confronted food shortages in terrible conditions and protested against these injustices.

As reform demands were not being met, a huge march was led by Georgy Astronovich, a priest. They marched to the Tsar's winter palace in St Petersburg. Many people were killed and injured when the troops of Tsar Nicholas II opened fire on the crowd. This became known to be Bloody Sunday.

After Bloody Sunday, there were riots in Russia.

The crew of the battleship Potemkin joined the revolt against the Tsar and mutinied on June 14th 1905 against their officers.

The Potemkin Mutiny

Nicholas promised to form a Dumas (parliament to workers) to advocate reforms for Russian workers.

Ten years passed before tensions in Russia rose again. Historians believe that the 1917 revolution began with the 1905 Riots and Bloody Sunday Massacre.

Nicholas II was under increasing pressure due to Japan's defeat during the Russo-Japanese War. He seemed more concerned for the problems in his home than the social or political crisis in his country. Nicholas believed that the Russian workers would not rebel against the monarchy despite Nicholas's son being seriously ill. He believed that the liberal members were fabricating the stories.

In the end it was only when the situation became worse that Nicholas was made to accept the October Manifesto. This manifesto was published in the fall of 1905. It stated that the entire population would be allowed vote and the Duma would allow workers to have a say in the government. Nicholas had to make all laws. This voice had no effect.

The Manifesto was drafted in an effort to save the country from revolution.

The outcome of World War One was to bring the situation to a boil, and it proved too much for the working classes.

1917 Revolution

Russia Entries WW1

The Russian Revolution was waged against Tsar Nicholas II in 1917. With the end to the monarchy, the path was open for the creation of the Soviet Union. There were not just one revolution, but two. The first revolution took place on February 28, 1917. The Tsar was made to relinquish his power and a provisional government was set up. This was to be a temporary solution, until the country becomes more stable.

The Bolsheviks or communists gained control in the October Revolution, also known as Red October.

Events that led to revolution

Russian society saw a significant shift when the peasants migrated to cities to work as factory workers. They came together in large numbers and began to complain of their terrible lives. Many of them were able to see that there was a way to improve their living situations by exercising their political muscles.

Most workers felt that change was coming with the Bloody Sunday Massacre as well as the creation of The Duma. It became clear quickly that the Duma had very limited power. The workers were very angry and vented all their anger on Nicholas II.

Russia joined the First World War in 1914. At first there was a surge for patriotism. The

Kaiser (king), along with his German troops, was the object of all this anger.

Russia was still a very poor state and the Russian soldiers were living in horrible conditions. Many soldiers didn't even possess guns. Russian soldiers were dying by thousands.

Nicholas took control and made a grave mistake. Again, the people blamed him for all the problems.

Nicholas was warned about revolution threat, but he chose not to take it seriously.

The February Revolution

The Revolution started when workers began to strike and refused work. There were protests over the lack of food. St Petersburg, the capital of Russia, was the scene of mass protests and factories were closed down.

Attacking Tsar's Police

Nicholas sent in troops, but many of his men joined the workers. The police also joined forces with the demonstrators. The government collapsed as there was no way to enforce its power.

Nicholas was forced on March 13 to abdicate. (Abdicate means to abdicate the throne.

The temporary government was in control of the situation.

From February to Oct

Conditions under the Provisional Administration didn't improve. Vladimir Lenin was a communist who returned from exile and settled in St Petersburg. He led a group called Bolsheviks. Bolsheviks had radical ideas based upon Karl Marx's works.

The Bolsheviks never thought they would be happy until their power was gained. The revolution started on October 10th. With little resistance, Bolsheviks were able to take over the government.

On October 25, Bolsheviks established a congress. Anybody who opposed Lenin were forced to resign. All other political parties were destroyed and the only government remaining was the Soviet,' which had Vladimir Lenin (the totalitarian leader) and Leon Trotsky (the sole representative).

It wasn't long before the Soviet prohibited private property, and the factories were handed over to workers.

Germany, Peace

Bolsheviks vowed to negotiate peace with the German Empire. This was done on 16th December 1917 when a cease fire was reached. The peace deal was signed in March 1918 with Russia handing large areas to Germany.

The Russian Civil War

The Red Army

Millions of Russians were killed and injured in civil wars that ensued after the October Revolution.

The civil conflict was between the Red Army Bolsheviks of the Bolsheviks & the Whites. The Whites were military commanders in the Tsar regime, as well socialists who opposed it but felt the Bolsheviks had become too extreme.

After the October Revolution in 1917, the Bolsheviks created an organized version the Red Army. This was an army that was made up mostly of the peasant class. These troops were against the Bolsheviks extreme policies and loathed the old Tsarist systems.

The Whites enjoyed the support and cooperation of all western powers, such as France, Great Britain, America, and others.

Vladimir Lenin, Bolshevik leader believed that the only solution to the old system was to establish a people's Army.

Reds versus Whites

The Russian Civil War ran from 1918 to1922. It was a struggle for control over the government, and it was between those Russians wanting a communist state and others who didn't. This conflict was fraught with chaos. Some people refused to return to the Tsar regime but believed that Bolsheviks are just as bad. These moderates weren't heard and were unfortunately not heard. Bolsheviks sought a society where all were equal, and that the government owned everything.

Because the Whites had military officers who had been trained to fight the Germans, it was assumed they would easily defeat the Red Army if they had the support of the West. This was not true. Bolsheviks promised bread for all who signed up. And millions of peasants began to flock to join their army.

Bolsheviks were more organised and had a simpler message that Russia's poorer citizens could understand.

They had a vision. The Whites wanted to return back to their old ways. The majority of poor Russians believed the vision of Lenin.

The three phases

In the first phase of the conflict, fighting was sporadic. It took place all across the country.

The second phase ran from November 1919 to December 1919. Although the Whites were prevailing in the conflict, Leon Trotsky organized the Red Army and made it more effective. They had superior numbers, and ultimately defeated the Whites.

The third phase consisted of the fight against Crimea. The White Army established its base in this region. However, once again, the Red Army's vast numbers of troops defeated them.

The USSR was formed on December 30, 1922. Russia was under the control and control of the Bolsheviks.

Around 8 million people died in the civil war. About one million were soldiers with the Red Army.

Many Russians succumbed to starvation.

The Red Army

Female Red Army Soldier

Bolshevik leaders realised that they required an army to remain in power after the revolution of 1917. The 1918 decree created the Red Army. It was made up of members of the peasant population in the country who had volunteered to help the new government. Leon Trotsky was the inventor of the army.

Trotsky recruited officers from his old Imperial Guard of The Tsar Imperial Guard to overcome the lack of military experience among the peasants. Trotsky did this because he didn't trust their loyalty. He appointed commissars as guardians to ensure that they were safe and also spread communist ideals to the troops.

In parallel, Bolshevik loyal officers were being trained as military officers and would eventually replace the older 'Tsarist' Officers.

Joseph Stalin assumed control over Russia's Red Army. Many Red Army officers were removed and only a few remained. However, this purge resulted in a decline in effectiveness and a drop in morale.

Red Army was dropped by the end World War Two.

1946. It was estimated that there were around 11 million Soviet troops.

In the following years, it fell to just over three million.

What is Communism and how can it be defined?

Karl Marx

Communism, a political movement that is founded on ideology, is called communism.

A communist is one who wants to live in an communist society and not in a capitalist state like America. The production of goods and common ownership would make this society possible. It would have no class system and money wouldn't be needed. This system has never been attempted in any country.

The state took ownership of the country's property after the fall of the Tsar. A small, elite group of people governed the country. There was only one political party that could be chosen, so there was no other political option to communism.

Communism represents a more extreme version of socialism.

Karl Marx wrote The Communist Manifesto, 1848 (Later Das Kapital). This document set out the foundational ideas for communism.

Marx said that communism's first step would be a period where there was change. The country would then be run by workers. The workers would now manage the production processes, and the state would take responsibility for each of its citizens. Marx was very vague about his theories because he believed that every country's workers had to decide what their concept of communism was.

There have been many attempts over the past century to establish communist nations. Russia was the first communist state to emerge, but China achieved a similar revolution back in the 1940s.

In 1960s America, around a quarter of the population was communist. Most of the countries followed Russian models.

In the 21stcentury, around 25% of the population still lives under communist rule. These include China and North Korea.

One of the problems with communism tends to be that it does not make everyone equally wealthy. In Russia for example, the ruling elite was replaced by a more brutal and equally violent one.

Vladimir Lenin (1870 - 1924)

Vladimir Lenin was chairman of the Soviet Union. He was born at Simbirsk (Russia) but died in Gorki during the formation of the Soviet Union.

Lenin's family was middle-class and his father was an educator. Lenin excelled academically and loved playing chess.

Lenin had just turned 16 when his father passed away and he was not yet sixteen when his brother was exiled by the Tsar's secret police as a revolutionary. These incidents had a significant effect on Lenin's entire life.

Lenin was studying at university when he began to be interested in politics. He believed Marxism was Russia's best choice.

He was graduated as a solicitor.

Lenin built a home for himself in St Petersburg and joined other Marxists there. Lenin founded the Bolsheviks Marxist Group in St Petersburg. Bolshevik literally means "One in the majority".

He was always aware about the secret police of The Tsar and all the spies living in the city. He was arrested on charges of revolutionary activity in 1897. He was sent to Siberia in prison camp for three years. He was also expelled from St Petersburg. He went to Western Europe after he was released. He was here he wrote many papers regarding Marxism. These were smuggled into Russia by the workers and then read by them. His writings focused upon the injustices of the Tsar as well as how revolution was the way to solve them. Many Russians were attracted to his views.

World War I

Many Russian peasants became soldiers to fight the Germans. Conditions on the eastern front were very difficult, and many died of starvation. They were no match for the German Army's highly-trained soldiers. Russian soldiers were poorly trained, had little food and were sometimes starving. The Russian Peasants were ready, willing and able to revolt against the Tsar.

The February Revolution

February 1917 saw revolution, which overthrew The Tsar. An interim government, based in the Duma, took over the government of the monarchist government.

Germans wanted Russia defeated so they could beat the British, French, American and other European powers. Lenin returned home to Russia and spoke out against their provisional government. Lenin claimed the were as bad and corrupt as the Tsar government.

The October Revolution

Lenin's Bolshevik Party overtook the government control in October 1917. Lenin established and led the Soviet Union.

Germany had agreed to Russia making peace. Lenin made this happen almost immediately. Lenin grabbed land owned by ruling classes and gave it to peasants.

The Russian Civil War

Lenin struggled to take control of Russia after ending the war in Germany. Anti-Bolshevik force (Whites), formed coalition and tried take back control.

Lenin was in need of a Red Army (Army of Peasants) to retain control.

Lenin won finally the civil battle and began to create laws to support the collapsed Russian economy.

Russia became the first communist world country with Lenin at its helm in 1922.

Lenin was gunned down in 1918, but he survived the assassination plot. His health began to decline as a result of the wounds. He suffered a stroke and died on January 21, 1924.

Trivia

Lenin is the father the Soviet Union. His ideas came to be known as Leninism and not Marxism. Lenin was without any doubt one the most influential leaders of 20th-century history.

Lenin didn't want Joseph Stalin succeeding him as leader. This was because he distrusted his motives

Nadya Kripskaya, also a revolutionary, was Lenin's spouse.

Leon Trotsky (1879 - 1940)

Leon Trotsky is one of the main planners who helped to drive the Russian Revolution forward in 1917. Trotsky was responsible for the Bolsheviks winning the civil war after defeating the Tsar. Without Trotsky's organizational skills, the revolution would not have been able to defeat the old Imperial Guard and power of west.

He was the child of Jewish parents.

He was highly intelligent and arrogant, which led to him having few friends at school. As a teenager, his involvement with anti-Tsar rebels was evident. He was 19 years old when he got arrested and was sent to Siberia. He managed to escape, and he made it to London.

Along with other Russian Revolutionists in London, he joined Lenin.

He returned to Russia in 1905 where he organized the first Soviet of St Petersburg. He was again held prisoner and sent back into

Siberia. He escaped again and made it to America.

Trotsky was able to return to Russia in May 1917 after having been in the USA and help the Bolsheviks defeat a Provisional Government. Trotsky knew that the Bolsheviks were to be protected against all of the forces that wanted their demise.

Trotsky arranged the Red Guard and made Peace with Germany.

After the revolution the Bolsheviks held only Moscow, Petrograd. They had no influence and were opposed to the rest.

Trotsky was made the Commissioner of War when the civil conflict broke out. Despite not having military training, Trotsky proved to be the right man and his Red Army defeated Bolsheviks. Trotsky/Lenin made a great team. Trotsky proved a brutal leader who wouldn't accept failure from his military officers. Trotsky was known as a close-knit commander in chief and traveled the country on his armored car.

The civil conflict was won in 1922. However, even though Trotsky was expected to be Lenin's successor it didn't happen.

Trotsky, because of his arrogance had many enemies. Joseph Stalin was the one to take control when Lenin died. Even though Lenin was against Stalin and saw him more as someone driven by power and greed, this was true.

Stalin expelled Trotsky (1927) from the Russian Communist party and exiled Trotsky (1929).

Trotsky's role in the killing of the Russian Royal Familie made it difficult for any country to accept Trotsky. He lived briefly in France, Turkey, and then in France for a time. In the end he decided to move to Mexico. There, a Stalinist assassin robbed him of his life in 1940.

Trotsky was ultimately defeated by the idea that there would be permanent revolution. He wanted Russia, to continue to export terror and to lead the world towards communism. Stalin, ironically since Russia was tired of revolution bloodshed by 1929, was considered a more moderate leader.

Joseph Stalin (1878-1953).

Joseph Stalin assumed control over the Soviet Union in 1924 after Vladimir Lenin passed away. Lenin advised against Stalin being given such a high post because he wasn't sure of his motives. Lenin was right at the end. Stalin was one world's most violent leaders, and millions of his subjects died during his time as president.

Stalin was brought up in Gori, Georgia. His family was poor and his childhood wasn't happy. He wanted the priesthood, but he was expelled from school for his revolutionary views towards the Tsar.

Yalta Summit - Roosevelt, Churchill and Stalin

Stalin joined Bolshevik Party. He was active as an organizer and robbed bank branches to finance the party.

Stalin was one of Lenin's key men when the Tsar was overthrown. Stalin became the leader of the Bolshevik party, and overtook Lenin. Leon Trotsky was included.

Stalin wanted to see the Soviet Union grow into an industrialized nation, so he built factories all across Russia.

He expelled anyone who disapproved of his policies. He set up labor camps in order to imprison political prisoners.

It is believed that Stalinism caused the death of between 20 to 40 million people.

Stalin created the Soviet Union as a ally with Germany during World War Two. Hitler, who was the German leader hating Stalin, broke the alliance, and sent his army over to the border.

Stalin allied against Germany with Britain (Churchill), America(Roosevelt), and Britain (Churchill).

After Germany was defeated the Soviet Union took control several Eastern European states and established a number of 'puppet' governments. This was also the beginning of the cold conflict between the Soviets (and the western powers).

Stalin died at Kuntsevo in Moscow on 5th March 1953.

The end of Romanov Family

Nicholas and his extended family (the Romanovs) were an immediate problem once the Bolsheviks had taken power. There were heated debates over whether execution or exile should be allowed.

Nicholas and Alexandra comprised the Russian Royal Families. There were four Romanov daughter: Olga. Anastasia. Maria. Tatiana. Alexei (the only son) was the heir and heir the throne. Nicholas loved his family so much that he was often distracted from affairs stateside. The Romanovs were a loving and happy family, including Alexandra as well as Nicholas.

The family moved to Yekaterinburg in the Ural Mountains. This was a strong anti-Tsar region.

The Tsar and all his relatives were killed on 16 juillet 1918. This was the end of three centuries-long rule by the Romanov Dynasty.

www.ingramcontent.com/pod-product-compliance
Lightning Source LLC
Chambersburg PA
CBHW050408120526
44590CB00015B/1884